on track ...

Hawkwind

every album, every song

Duncan Harris

sonicbondpublishing.com

on track ...

Hawkwind

every album, every song

Duncan Harris

sonicbondpublishing.com

Sonicbond Publishing Limited
www.sonicbondpublishing.co.uk
Email: info@sonicbondpublishing.co.uk

First Published in the United Kingdom 2020
First Published in the United States 2020

British Library Cataloguing in Publication Data:
A Catalogue record for this book is available from the British Library

ISBN 978-1-78952-052-1

Typeset in ITC Garamond & ITC Avant Garde
Printed and bound in England

Graphic design and typesetting: Full Moon Media

For Sammie, who joined me on this great adventure
and, thankfully, loves to see Hawkwind live.

on track ... Hawkwind

Contents

Contents by Album

Continued overleaf

Contents by album

Acknowledgements

The author thanks the current band, particularly Dave and Kris Brock, Vicky Powell at Atomhenge and everyone involved with Hawkwind past and present.

Many thanks to Chris Walkden for his fine live pictures and a huge thank you to Stephen Lambe for allowing me to make my appreciation of the mighty Hawkwind known to the world.

Author's Note

Hawkwind have released a mountain of official studio and live albums. In addition, there have been a plethora of 'grey area' and bootleg albums that are, at best, only marginally worthwhile. This book will cover the main studio albums but will also include the three major live albums that have done the most to cement Hawkwind's majestic reputation. In order to prove itself as useful as possible, this book attempts to arrive at definitive statements concerning band personnel, songwriters and other information concerning the band. All songwriters are listed purely in alphabetical order. In addition, several songs have appeared under different names, e.g. 'Hassan I Sabbah' is often quoted as 'Assassins Of Allah'. Correct titles are noted [in square brackets] in the text.

I have taken a rather individual view of what constitutes a Hawkwind album: discounting 2000s *Spacebrock* (as it is just a Dave Brock solo album in a very penetrable disguise) and the Psychedelic Warriors trio side project *White Zone* but including Robert Calvert's nominally solo outing *Captain Lockheed and the Starfighters*, the Hawkwind Light Orchestra's *Stellar Variations* and the Hawklords album *25 Years On*. The reasons for this will become clear later.

Introduction

Inner space as much as outer space

Early Hawkwind is the sound of musical Barbarians at the gate and, apart from their aberrant 'Silver Machine' single, they have never been allowed into the mainstream. Often their outsider status has been physical as well as a state of mind. Jimi Hendrix dedicated a song to 'the cat with the silver face' at the 1970 Isle Of Wight Festival, and that 'cat' turned out to be Nik Turner, founding member of Hawkwind, who had painted his face with silver stars and was playing several free gigs outside the festival wall with the band in protest at the high ticket prices.

As well as being renowned for playing free gigs and festivals Hawkwind were also initially infamous for their lack of musicianship. Most of the early band members were people who had taught themselves to play instruments (Nik Turner, Dik Mik). Some were solid players, but their ideal gig was to turn up, play a freeform psychedelic rock jam (usually entitled 'Sunshine Special') for one or two hours straight through, without any breaks for applause, and then leave to a standing ovation. The band was inspired by the avant-garde elements of Pink Floyd but also cite the vast Krautrock movement (particularly Amon Duul II, Can and Neu) nascent in Germany at the time.

While bands come and go, the name Hawkwind carries on, producing striking music and almost representing an entire lifestyle. Always enigmatic and outside of the mainstream most people associate Hawkwind with 'whoosh' noises, 'Silver Machine', Lemmy and the occasional recognition that they produce something called Space Rock music. Even from the cursory glance afforded by this book it will be clear that there is far more to this group than this long-lived but inaccurate stereotype. Hawkwind's longevity can be ascribed to both luck and determination, but part of the secret of their long life is that they actively accept and promote change both musically and, inevitably, in personnel.

Perhaps surprisingly one of the band's early stated aims was to create an atmosphere for the audience combining music, lights, dance, theatre and mime that was psychedelic and tripped out *without* the need for illegal drugs of any kind. Most of the band members dabbled if I can be politic, in hallucinogenic drugs to one extent or another, and the tales of the band's drug intake are legendary. This has to be looked at in context, of course: the principal drug of the day, LSD, had only been criminalised by Parliament in 1966 and many people had carried on using it, particularly when it seemed that other bands had continued to use only recently illegal drugs themselves.

The band officially came together in late 1969 as Group X – mostly because they couldn't think of a name for themselves and they had a gig that night. John Peel saw them and recommended to Doug Smith that he sign a management deal with the band there and then. The band continued looking for a name and settled on Hawkwind Zoo. With that settled they recorded their first demo, consisting of three songs, and Doug Smith began hawking it around various major labels. Almost immediately the nascent Hawkwind signed contracts with Andrew Lauder's Liberty label, under the name Hawkwind Zoo. However, before another note could be recorded, founding guitarist Mick Slattery suddenly departed for Morocco with wanderlust triumphing over the music. In order to record an album, the band felt they required a new lead guitarist. In keeping with the times, they found one easily, a startlingly adept soloist in the form of Huw Lloyd-Langton, and they were back on the road.

At the same time, the band was attracting interest from other Ladbroke Grove/Notting Hill creative people. Michael Moorcock, even then an iconic SF/fantasy/literary author, was invited by South African-born poet and writer Robert Calvert to come to a Group X free concert, and meet the group, and both were struck by the band's chaotic maelstrom of sound. Moorcock characterised them by suggesting 'they were like the mad crew of a long-distance spaceship who had forgotten the purpose of their mission...'

Doug Smith ran the new name past John Peel who suggested dropping the 'Zoo' part as he felt it was too American, 'to Haight Ashbury.' Thus christened they entered a studio with The Pretty Things' guitarist Dick Taylor as producer, to record their debut album.

The real Hawkwind

Over the years, many spurious and highly amusing explanations have been given for the Hawkwind name ranging from the daft to the sublime. The perpetuation of various myths has always been part of the band's psychology, but with the advent of two detailed biographies, the truth has re-emerged. Hawkwind are so named because of Nik Turner. He was, and still is, infamous for his incessant farting (the 'wind') and frequent bouts of hawking up phlegm and spitting it out (the 'hawk'). Spurred on by Michael Moorcock's Hawkmoon character the band shuffled the words around and a band name was born. It helps that Nik possesses a hawk-like nose and that the hawk is both an ancient Egyptian and pagan symbol, but the fact of the matter is that farting named this band!

A Hawkwind overview

Hawkwind are underground in more ways than one. In a remarkably familiar situation to many other bands, they are most famous for a song that they dislike and which doesn't reflect the main musical thrust of the band. 'Silver Machine' may be the only familiar piece that the general public has ever heard. This is unfortunate because, even at the time, it was regarded as a joke and, apparently, overdubbed as if it was a stereotypical Hawkwind song.

This is a shame, because the band, and Brock, in particular, have produced some of the finest rock songs of the past half-century: songs that should be famous: songs that should be all over rock radio and played by today's buskers. 'Master Of The Universe', 'Brainstorm', 'Urban Guerilla', 'Assault and Battery', 'Quark, Strangeness and Charm', 'Hassan I Sabbah', 'Night Of The Hawks',

'Needle Gun', 'Right To Decide' and 'Love In Space' are all superbly written, largely concise and certainly innovative rock songs with playful and exciting lyrics that deserve to be heard. As it is Hawkwind have to rely upon their undoubted influence on generations of new groups to see their legacy live on. Describing Hawkwind has always been a tricky proposition. Originally, they were part of the underground, at whose head strode Pink Floyd, but they never really fitted into the categories that followed. Various magazines make a case for them as progressive rock, but their attitude, lack of ability and musical style somewhat precludes that description. Hawkwind followed the Krautrock path of repetition and riffs rather than the intricacies, musicality and perceived bombast of the major progressive rock bands. It's fair to say that Hawkwind have almost nothing in common with ELP, Yes, Genesis and their ilk although a resemblance to early Pink Floyd experimentation is sometimes apparent. No, Hawkwind's free-playing, people's band mantle and brutally aggressive musicianship had much more resonance with Punk Rock when it arrived. It's no coincidence that artists as diverse as Chrome, The Sex Pistols, Dead Kennedys and Monster Magnet have all acknowledged the profound influence the band have had on them. Sometimes musically and sometimes in attitude Hawkwind have a pervasive influence that belies their sales figures. Hawkwind stand as a testament to the power of the repeated, and repeated, and repeated, and repeated, and repeated riff and the joy of musical chaos and for much of that time they have been lead by one man:

Dave Brock, the Captain

Although difficult to isolate the precise time it's become pretty clear that Dave Brock took much of the control of the musical entity Hawkwind somewhere around 1972 with, ironically, the success of 'Silver Machine'. By co-penning their biggest hit and writing the bulk of their material at that time, he was able to declare himself as the Captain of Spaceship Hawkwind. There is nothing inherently wrong with this. The majority opinion seems to be that most bands need a leader or a dictator. Groups that rely on collective composition tend to end up in self-indulgent backwaters, exploring musical blind alleys or exploding into several pieces, all of which have afflicted Nik Turner's various musical endeavours.

The problem that has always faced Dave Brock is that some people believe he took the reins because he wanted that control. Brock, and others suggest that someone had to take charge and, as nobody else volunteered to do it, he stepped in. Whichever is correct and, I suspect, both motivations can be interpreted as the truth, Dave Brock has undoubtedly set himself up as the figurehead (and therefore target) for anyone who wishes to throw brickbats at the band. An argument could be made that Brock wanted to control the musical direction of the band but, given his extensive songwriting contributions, that would have happened naturally anyway.

After the gradual sidelining and then ousting (and occasional reinstatement) of co-founder Nik Turner in 1976, the band have only ever had the one continuous rock around which the band revolves, Dave Brock. It should be noted that during the labyrinthine internecine battles that occurred in 1976 even Brock was sacked from the band which suggests that his control of the band was far less than is claimed by some.

Intriguingly it seems that Brock actually works better in collaboration with others. From the formation of the band to around 1976 the band played largely as a collective, with some strong musical personalities coming to the fore. After Turner's dismissal, it became the Robert Calvert and Dave Brock group, which didn't last too long given Calvert's ongoing mental health issues. From 1979 until 1989 the pairing involved Brock and Huw Lloyd Langton, although it is arguable that Alan Davey's contribution from 1984-1996 could be seen as superseding Lloyd Langton's role. Brock, it seems, has always needed a strong bass player to really anchor his own playing. Dave Anderson was both creative and impressive but didn't last long. Lemmy, of course, was Brock's undoubted musical soul-mate and often commented upon the fact that he shared an almost telepathic connection with Brock that he was never able to replicate. Brock, in return, says that 'there was a magic between us. Some of the best times I had were with Lemmy in the band.'

Now, of course, Dave Brock has earned the right to call himself the Captain and has presided over 50 years of an active Hawkwind which has left a prodigious body of work and one that deserves celebration and recognition.

The politics of Hawkwind

Whether the political philosophy of anarchism was introduced to the band by Michael Moorcock (a respected and committed speaker about the subject) or whether he was attracted to them because of their unconscious anarchism is unclear, but the end result is a band that has, by example, shown their clear anarchist tendencies. Playing for free, organising their own festivals, guesting with other people, shedding and gaining members almost at random and constantly pushing at their own boundaries has given the band a large black flag following.

Throughout the years though it has become apparent that Hawkwind have represented one core vision more than any other, whoever was writing words for them. Hawkwind, and by this I mean the collective entity rather than any individual, see the future as essentially dystopian. In short, the world is going to Hell. Ruined cities, starvation, unemployment, plagues, environmental disaster, mental breakdown, global warming, the death of people, the death of planets, the stark emptiness of space, the belief that the Universe is essentially hostile and the terror of no longer being human have permeated the vast bulk of 50 years worth of recordings. A song on every album, sometimes *whole* albums, are dedicated to the underlying theme that the Earth and its people are doomed unless we make changes and improve ourselves before it all ends.

Given the variety of writers (Robert Calvert, Nik Turner, Lemmy, Dave

Brock, Michael Moorcock, Huw and Marion Lloyd Langton, Alan Davey to mention a few) it is surprising that there is such a consistency in the point of view and such devotion to a central idea. Space and science fiction may be their overriding fixations, but it's a blackness of heart and soul as well as the darkness of space that truly sets them apart.

1: Dawn of the Hawks (1969-1970)

Having come from a busking blues and jug band background the advent of Pink Floyd, Arthur Brown and Jimi Hendrix fired Dave Brock with a desire to follow a more psychedelic musical path and the concurrent beginnings of a large German musical scene, later dubbed Krautrock by the UK music press, all siphoned into the sound of Brock's as yet ill-defined new musical venture. Brock continued, however, to busk to maintain some sort of income as he was already married with a child.

Early live appearances were legendary, not only for their sax and riffs and rock'n'roll music but also the primitive use of lights and backdrops that would come to fruition only a few years later. Live is where the band clicked, and it attracted the attention of future band members, DJs, future managers and a great deal of the Ladbroke Grove intelligentsia.

Still, before that, they had the little matter of Mick Slattery's desertion, the recruitment of Huw Lloyd-Langton, and the recording of their debut album to contend with.

Hawkwind (Liberty, August 1970)

Personnel:
Dave Brock: vocals, guitars, harmonica, percussion
John Harrison: bass guitar
Huw Lloyd Langton: lead guitar
Terry Ollis: drums
Nik Turner: saxophone, vocals, percussion
Dik Mik: electronics
Dick Taylor: lead and back-up guitars (uncredited)
Produced at Trident Studios, London, April 1970 by Dick Taylor and Hawkwind.
Highest chart place: 75 (UK)
Running time (approximate): 39:40

In the studio for the first time, the band wanted to keep everything simple for their debut album. Given their relative inexperience, the band have all given due credit to Dick Taylor (guitarist for late '60s almost-seminal group The Pretty Things) for creating songs from the chaos. The band had played-in their single, hour-long, song live for months beforehand, and essentially played their live set in the studio three or four times. Then they picked the take they liked the best and tarted it up with a bit of musical spit and polish. The band had six recording days and spent, according to several sources, three of the days on 'Hurry on Sundown' alone. 'Mirror of Illusion' had time spent on it too. Looking back the reason is obvious: these were the two most commercial songs and were slated as the single release to promote the album.

Uniformly the band members of the time are proud of their debut and look back on it with fond memories. From an outsider's point of view, it has its problems. In essence, the album is bookended by two songs and, in the middle, is a single sprawling piece of experimentation, soloing, improvisation, avant-garde sax, audio generator effects and free form rock split into four parts and given random titles. These twenty-eight minutes actually comprise a somewhat edited version of the hour-long 'Sunshine Special' song broken up into smaller bite-size parts, with occasional additional overdubs.

'Hurry On Sundown' (Dave Brock)

If you are going to set out your stall as the prime psychedelic experimentalists of the UK, then the best place to start is with a winsome and startlingly melodic, folk/busking hybrid that bears no relation to the rest of the music that is about to explode in your ears. It starts with nicely jaunty twelve-string guitar picking and a minor chord before moving into a bluesy harmonica part and a rock-steady bass high in the mix, combining with a relaxed lead guitar (almost definitely from producer Dick Taylor); the song then rolls along in sprightly fashion arriving at a sweet chorus melody and a surprisingly disappointing singles chart position. The lyrics clearly drip with hippie anti-war platitudes and suffer from bland repetition. It is a straight, frankly commercial, blues-tinged folk song with a lot to recommend it in the musical department. Needless to say, it isn't representative of the band.

Astonishingly it was inspired by the twee folk trio Peter, Paul & Mary and their song 'Hurry Sundown' (from the album *See What Tomorrow Brings*: can you see what Brock did there...) – this is hummable busking material at its zenith. No longer lightweight and faintly desperate, as the earlier demo shows, this song sees the invention of busking psychedelia which went on to spawn future Dave Brock epics like 'We Took The Wrong Step Years Ago', 'Down Through The Night' and 'The Demented Man' before disappearing from the band's musical repertoire almost entirely.

Having virtually defined catchy psychedelic folk, the group immediately abandoned the style for more free-form fare; a studio rendering of the sprawling and partially improvised 'Sunshine Special':

'The Reason Is?' (Hawkwind)

'The Reason Is?', like all great sonic experiments, starts with a shimmering gong strike (echoing Pink Floyd and, ahem, the group Gong) and then plunges the listener headlong into an area previously only inhabited by German bands like Amon Duul I & Amon Duul II and doesn't let up for almost half an hour. Although it undoubtedly says 3.30 on the cover, the following four songs are all parts of the same over-arching piece, as evidenced by the real lack of any breaks in the music, until 'Mirror of Illusion'. Here 'The Reason Is?' proceeds to provide ethereal voices, wind effects, endlessly circling cymbals and a brief bass throb introduction before it mutates into:

'Be Yourself' (Hawkwind)

Opening with a heavy bass and guitar riff before stumbling into a brief section of stentorian vocals exhorting you to, unsurprisingly, 'be yourself', its' simple repetitive rhythms and chords disappear, only to be replaced by the first sign of Nik Turner's saxophone on the album over tumbling drums. This leads to a rather fine guitar solo (also likely to be Taylor's work) and then it returns to the foghorn vocals before suffering a mini-musical breakdown which inevitably leads into:

'Paranoia (Part 1)'/'**Paranoia** (Part 2)' (Hawkwind)

The short musical vignette of Part 1 is a ham-fisted Black Sabbath-like doom riff, only halted by the end of the original vinyl LP side getting in the way, illustrated by the winding down of the music as if the turntable is slowing. The game is given away completely when Part 2 restarts on the flip-side and sounds much the same as its earlier counterpart, only with an introduction of deep bass, more swirling cymbals, Brock exhorting everyone to get 'higher' and the blunderbuss return of the main riff to proceedings. Finally, here, Dik Mik's electronics really come to the fore as he makes the sound of whip cracks and synthesised attempts at imitating a theremin. Without stopping (although it does slow down as it nears the end, as with Part 1) the piece goes directly on to:

'Seeing It As You Really Are' (Hawkwind)

Beginning as a slowly drifting miasma of electronic effects and the ever-present cymbals and wordless voices this part finds Turner mostly sitting out on the saxophone but apparently contributing the improvised vocals instead. Huw Lloyd Langton undoubtedly has a moment to shine on the guitar solo, but this quickly devolves into the sound of screaming and a pounding final section that, at last, highlights the forthcoming Hawkwind 'sound'. By the time 'Seeing It as You Really Are' ends the experimental section, it's clear that the band have explored this musical blind alley to its limits. They would go on to use a lot of the ideas and atmospheres in forthcoming albums but they would do it with greater aplomb and a modicum of succinctness.

'Mirror of Illusion' (Brock)

A sound like a rattlesnake and then a basic guitar jangle greets the listener for the final song on the album. Plastering on electronic noises from the audio generator and imitating the theremin again can't disguise the fundamental busking/folk nature of the song. Not as supremely catchy as 'Hurry on Sundown', and featuring a clunky demo-quality guitar sound and quirky percussion fade-out, it nevertheless has a shiny commerciality to its melodic vocals that belies its weak instrumentation. The sound of Lloyd Langton's delicately melodic lead guitar is a welcome relief from the somewhat aimless previous half-hour. No wonder it was the single's b-side.

Lyrically Brock presents an early warning of the dangers of drugs with couplets like:

> And the dream-world that you've found
> Will one day drag you down
> The mirror of illusion reflects the smile

That 'smile' is more akin to the Joker from *Batman* than any sign of happiness. Brock then specifically identifies the psychedelics, apparently so prevalent in the band at that time by saying:

> You think you've found perception's doors
> They open to a lie

Although William Blake coined the phrase 'the doors of perception' in his poem 'The Marriage of Heaven and Hell' it became widely disseminated by Aldous Huxley's book *The Doors of Perception*; an account of Huxley's psychedelic experiences on Mescaline, a naturally occurring hallucinogenic, which has comparable effects to LSD and psilocybin (the active ingredient of magic mushrooms) in its mind-altering properties. Hawkwind gained notoriety later on for their apparent over-indulgent drug use, but lyrically this virtually pre-dates the group and certainly comes before the band's hedonistic drug culture defined their early 1970s image. Ironically, the band claim on the sleeve of their debut that:

> We started out trying to freak people (trippers), now we are trying to levitate their minds, in a nice way, without acid, with ultimately a complete audio-visual thing. Using a complex of electronics, lights and environmental experiences.

Twenty-two years later Brock would resurrect this song, retitled 'Mask of Morning', and while the musical setting was completely re-tooled, he retained almost the entire vocal melody and, in passing, demonstrated that his voice had barely changed over the decades.

Hawkwind Zoo Bonus Tracks

Given the extraordinarily tight recording schedule, it came as a surprise to be presented, over 40 years later, with the original recording of 'You Know You're Only Dreaming' from the debut album sessions. All shouted vocals, strummed acoustic guitars and propelled by wildly thrashing drums the avant-garde breakdown into a 'Sunshine Special' musical quotation at around the three-minute mark makes this early version of the song from *X In Search Of Space* a very different beast indeed. Dave Brock pulls the piece out of the morass after a few minutes to return to the lyrics, but it's a losing battle to find a decent song amongst the confused structure and disappointing vocals.

Although recorded as demo songs in 1969, the Hawkwind Zoo bonus tracks give a schizophrenic impression of the band at the time. 'Kiss of the Velvet Whip' (aka 'Sweet Mistress Of Pain') is a blatant S&M themed song that points to other, more radical, lyrical destinations that the band could have pursued but wisely never did. Musically it is a basic rock thrash-about (with a disarmingly pretty guitar introduction) which puts frantic guitar, blaring sax and pounding drums ahead of a decent melody or a sense of brevity. The song is about two minutes and several lyrical repeats too long. In a somewhat strange move, the band re-recorded the song in 1971, extending and rearranging it to fit in with the changed band dynamic of the era. Although better produced the song still retains its aberrant (and possibly abhorrent) lyrics. Nik Turner plasters sax all over the cracks, but this remains a disappointing slog around that wouldn't have added to the majestic *X In Search Of Space* one iota.

Most illuminating of the Hawkwind Zoo demos is the version of Pink Floyd's 'Cymbaline' which, as a song, was intentionally left off the debut album in order for the band to forge their own sound rather than saddle themselves with endless comparisons. Dave Brock handles the vocals well, the song sounds just as lush and ethereal as the original, but the production is definitely demo quality with the drums rather over-shadowing the mix.

2: Day of the Hawks (1971-1975)

After the relative success of their debut, the band quickly drew in new talent and new creativity. Their next album was designed to cement both their reputation and their mythological background. To that end, the band insisted on taking into the fold the pneumatic and statuesque Stacia who spent much of her time dancing semi-naked (usually covered in stars and body paint) in front of newly installed Liquid Len's lights, while Robert Calvert and designer extraordinaire Barney Bubbles were concocting a complete visual package for the next album release which was going to include a 24-page booklet combining pictures, lyrics and words into a cohesive conceptual springboard for the band's future excursions. The Hawkwind Log was a milestone, and the creative spirit around the band was just getting into its stride.

So it came as some surprise that bassist John Harrison parted company with the band soon after, apparently at his own request. The band quickly drafted in Thomas Crimble of Skin Alley, who shared Hawkwind's management. With Crimble, they played outside the gates of the 1970 Isle of Wight festival for free and, soon after, lost guitarist Huw Lloyd Langton due to an LSD spiked orange juice that caused a nervous breakdown and a period of retreat for the shy Welshman. The death of Jimi Hendrix at around the same time also gave the band pause for thought at the then pervasive drug culture surrounding the group. On top of that, it appeared that things weren't working out with Crimble and he was invited to leave in the December of 1970.

Dave Anderson had been a pivotal member of West German band Amon Duul II but left them, amicably, because he didn't want to live in Germany for the rest of his life. He had returned to London on the lookout for work and had stand-in positions for a couple of groups before he replaced Nic Potter in darkly experimental group Van Der Graaf Generator. By all accounts his tenure was short (it may have been as short as a week!) but he was in the perfect place to jump on the Hawkwind ship.

Around the same time Dik Mik had been thinking about leaving the band after a car crash that he'd been involved in so, in order to smooth the way in case he did leave, they simply promoted their tour manager, Del Dettmar, to the possibly vacant audio generator and synthesizer stool. As it turned out, Dik Mik had a change of heart, so another extra member was added.

Along with the visually arresting dancing of six-foot Amazon Stacia (and both she and Terry Ollis would often perform gigs in the nude), Hawkwind's rough patch turned into a blessing in disguise.

X In Search Of Space (United Artists, October 1971)

Personnel:
Dave Brock: vocals, guitars, audio generator
Dave Anderson: bass guitar, guitars
Terry Ollis: drums, percussion

Nik Turner: saxophone, flute, audio generator, vocals
Del Dettmar: synthesizer
Dik Mik: audio generator
Produced at Olympic Studios, London and Air Studios, London, July 1971 by Hawkwind and George Chkiantz.
Highest chart place: 18 (UK)
Running time (approximately): 42:22

Barney Bubbles masterminded an intricate fold-out sleeve for the cover and, along with the Hawkwind Log, created an image for the band that lives on today. The most surprising artistic statement, aside from the difficulty of making the fold-out cover in the first place, is the densely packed 24-page Hawkwind Log that accompanies the album. Poems, stories and artwork combine, as a mythology is built for the band. It includes words that would later be used as lyrics for 'Spirit of the Age' and others.

During the recording of the album, Robert Calvert became an official member of the band and, when he was incapacitated for whatever reason, Michael Moorcock would fill in for him in live situations. Opting to produce themselves, they initially started work at George Martin's Air Studios, but acid-spiked drinks again caused problems and put paid to their stay. Once at Olympic studios, however, they worked quickly and recorded efficiently.

'You Shouldn't Do That' (Brock/Nik Turner)

Opening with the electronic tinkering of Dik Mik and Del Dettmar, Hawkwind announce their sophomore presence to the world with a fifteen-minute distillation of their entire improvised oeuvre. With the sound of a spacecraft ascending to the heavens the band then throw in a sturdy bassline, squalling sax and flailing drums. The sax becomes a tiny bit more melodic as the song unfolds, although the audio generator sounds continue to interrupt with high register squeaks and swirling ascents and descents. 'You Shouldn't Do That' has learned that quiet and loud are two separate things, Turner provides much more sax than previously, the noises and percussion are mind-blowing, and the sibilant hiss of the title chant contributes to a classic but extremely experimental opening track. Brock whispers the chant while Turner sings roughshod over the top with lines like:

You want so hard to get somewhere
With trees and flowers growing there
You try so hard to get somewhere
They put you down and cut your hair
You're trying to fly, you get nowhere
You get no air, you're getting aware

... which is hardly Shakespeare but it is the cumulative effect of the twin vocals, the battering rhythm and the constant sonic assault of the audio generators that really make this song. Based around a simplistically moronic rhythm, arguably initiated by Dave Anderson but utilising the chunky rhythm guitar of Brock to marvellous effect, this song distils the group jams of the debut album into one fifteen-minute mass of riffing and chanting that caused the end of further improvisations because they had taken the concept as far as they could.

In view of its startlingly easy format, it isn't a surprise that Hawkwind work the song into many others as a bridge or play small sections of it to lead into other songs. The incessant repetition of the piece throughout their career lends a certain credence to the idea that Hawkwind have actually played just one single song for 50 years.

'You Know You're Only Dreaming' (Brock)

Illustrating the remarkable integration of psychedelic effects (complete with flutes passed through effects pedals and honking sax all over) into the central busking core of the song, it's a delight to hear an uncluttered arrangement that highlights the underlying song. The electronic opening is rather more guitar-led than previously, but the presence of a vocal melody and the 'oohs' of backing vocals give the song a strange hybrid quality when it goes into a rather more free-form section later on which fades out with guitar and electronics washes several minutes later.

An argument can be made that this song is continued in 'We Took The Wrong Step Years Ago', both lyrically and musically. Brock has mentioned on several occasions that the early band would record hour-long jams live in the studio and then chop up the resulting morass into more recognisable songs, adding overdubs as needed, and this could be an example of this method of working.

'Master Of The Universe' (Brock/Turner)

Of course, this is the jewel here, its huge chugging chunky riff and its slithering and sliding guitar washes powering up and winding down make it seem more like a force of nature than a song. Brock's rhythm guitar takes centre stage briefly and then combines with the monumental bass riff to create the sound of tectonic plates moving. The phasing added to the riff later in the song merely makes it sound like the whole thing was designed to move planets. The lyrics, along with most of the album are inspired by the mythology being produced all around them. This is the song Lemmy has gone on record as wishing he had written (he would ultimately cannibalise the bass line, rhythm and song progression for Motorhead's own 'Deaf Forever' in 1986). The definitive Hawkwind song, this is a conscious exploration of their own self-made mythology. Turner, with input and editing from Calvert, speaks of the power of music and the power of the universe in the same breath. Swirling through space, both literal and metaphorical, the band speed up and slow down almost alchemically.

Anderson waited 30 years to claim a credit on this song, putting it somewhat outside any statute of limitations, citing the barre chords as his unique contribution and insisting that he had to teach Brock how to play the chords required. Brock, on the other hand, seems convinced that the music is his while the lyrics are Turner's. Musically there does appear to be a similarity to the Anderson/Turner credited 'Children Of The Sun', but then Brock has also produced songs that utilise barre chords, so the argument is somewhat moot at this point. The song itself remains a live fixture for all the permutations.

The song seems to have invented space rock all on its own.

'We Took The Wrong Step Years Ago' (Brock)

Brock starts with a folky 12 string acoustic guitar and the cries of gulls before regaling us with an early tale of environmental catastrophe and a vocal doused in world-weary regret. The band sympathetically open out the mid-section, maintaining the acoustic nature of the track, before it returns to its melodic core. The electronic swoops and swooshes merely add to the presence this little jewel possesses. This is a remarkable song from a young band, and it's most remarkable for its lyrical prescience and musically catchy beauty.

An astonishing 47 years later a very different Hawkwind would return to the song with a stunning and lushly orchestrated rearrangement, complete with a string section, oboe and flute solo that makes it sound like a lost treasure from Nick Drake's early solo albums, on 2018's otherwise poorly received *Road to Utopia*. Surprisingly, Brock's voice appears in better form than the 1971 original.

'Adjust Me' (Hawkwind)

In an early precursor to future album track listings there follows a madly eclectic piece of avant-garde music from the whole band towards the end of the album. The band appear to throw a bunch of unused riffs into a pot and then stand well back while each band member jams something unconventional on top. Calling this a song is debatable although it does have song-like qualities at times. The sped-up finale is a saving grace, but this definitely outstays its welcome given its 5:46 running time. The lyrics are short and suggest that the band are going a little crazy in the studio.

'Children Of The Sun' (Dave Anderson/Turner)

The clunky blow-out of 'Adjust Me' is neatly counter-pointed by the alluring acoustic darkness and floating flute of this entrancing tune. A clear strum-along end-piece this track finishes the album on a semi-serene note, its' somewhat jerky rhythm notwithstanding. Dave Anderson actually wrote the music for this, after he had officially departed the band, simply because the album was five minutes short...

Anderson was leaving Hawkwind even before the recording sessions began. Whether due to antagonism with Brock or personality clashes with the whole band, a sudden and career prevailing preference for the studio environment over the punishing live performance schedule or simply a desire to tackle America that the rest of the band appeared to decline, Anderson made up his mind to leave.

Enter, stage right, rock icon and bass God in waiting, Ian 'Lemmy' Kilmister, hereafter referred to, simply, as Lemmy. A jobbing rhythm guitarist and singer, Lemmy had paid his dues by becoming a roadie for Jimi Hendrix before joining (and then writing much of the material for) tabla player Sam Gopal's Dream. Lemmy's introduction to Hawkwind was yet another gruelling tour. He had never played bass before and the switch from rhythm guitar gave his bass playing an unconventional lead instrument quality. It cemented his reputation as both a serious rock and roll musician and the Godfather of punk. Lemmy is a legend and for all practical purposes, it starts here. He was the second member of the speed (amphetamine sulphate) contingent, along with Dik Mik, and that set him apart from the largely dope and acid (LSD) fuelled majority in the band. The kinetic energy and metallic sound he brought to the band encouraged the other members to reach further heights.

Terry Ollis, on the other hand, while continuing to drum wildly, and oftentimes nakedly, was becoming a serious problem. As well as failing to show up for several gigs, on other occasions he could be found slumped over his drum kit not playing anything at all. Terry Ollis, it seemed, was the latest to succumb to the lure of drugs. On the back of various last-minute substitutions (Viv Prince of The Pretty Things, Twink of The Pink Fairies) the band looked for a new, dependable, drummer.

Simon King was already known as a player in Opal Butterfly and, in essence, became the back-up drummer for a little while. When Terry Ollis couldn't take part, Simon King took over. This short stint culminated in Terry Ollis' sacking. Both drummers were playing with Hawkwind at a London concert when it was noticed that Ollis couldn't keep time and kept slowing down. While the band has a certain tolerance, they also have a desire to present a consistently impressive live show, and Ollis broke the camel's back on this occasion.

Ollis was out, King was in and thus was created the seminal band line-up. The first order of business, as ever, was touring. This time, however, there was a difference. The Roundhouse, February 13th 1972, was the scene of the Greasy Truckers Party charity gig. Although Lemmy and Dik Mik had to be helped on stage due to their prodigious drug intake, the band performed a storming gig, and it was recorded for posterity. Strangely, chopped up parts of it would appear on three separate compilation albums before the entire, unadulterated, concert was finally released in all its glory in 2007, 35 years after its original recording.

'Silver Machine' (Brock/Robert Calvert)

The most famous Hawkwind song is a satirical attack on actual songs about space travel, concerning - as it does - a bicycle. Calvert had noted Alfred Jarry's 1900 essay 'How To Construct A Time Machine' and quickly understood that it was a metaphor describing the author's bike. Jarry was notorious for cycling around Paris while armed with two pistols and Calvert was excited to create a legendary spoof because of it.

No-one disputes the authorship of the song, but many will find it credited to Calvert/MacManus on early appearances. This was a deliberate ploy on Brock's behalf to persuade the music publishers to give the actual songwriters increased royalties (MacManus being his wife's maiden name).

The music, once the swirling, fluttering synthesizers and solid bass are removed, turns out to be somewhat bland rock and roll more suited to the 1950s than the 1970s. Brock's music is perfunctory at best, but it's the embellishments that enable the song to live on. The graduation from album filler to hit single, however, involved a hefty amount of re-recording, tweaking and overdubbing. Recognising that the song was both a fairly concise musical statement and that it had a certain melodic brutality, meant that the record company, the band and their manager could work up the song into something single-worthy. The first things that went were the leaden and garbled vocals of Robert Calvert. Suffering from the beginnings of a mental breakdown, Calvert sang somewhat out of tune: the vocals proved to be the biggest stumbling block for the band. The rather rambling song was edited, treated, beefed up in the mix and extra electronic effects were added to create the pithy song the band had been looking for. Unfortunately, they couldn't find the right singer. By all accounts, both Brock and Turner had a go but Calvert, having been sectioned for 28 days under Mental Health legislation, was busy in hospital suffering from nervous exhaustion and couldn't make another pass at singing. In desperation, they tried Lemmy and, according to all reports, he nailed it within two or three takes to produce the commercial zenith we all know today.

The single was released in June 1972, and the surprise success meant that an album needed to accompany it fairly quickly. The money generated by the single also allowed the band to stretch out financially on their stage show. In came more lights, extra dancers, strobe effects and both painted equipment and backdrops. The band was on a roll.

Doremi Fasol Latido (United Artists, November 1972)

Personnel:
Dave Brock: vocals, guitars
Lemmy: bass guitar, guitar, vocals
Simon King: drums, percussion
Nik Turner: saxophone, flute, vocals
Del Dettmar: synthesizer
Dik Mik: audio generators, electronics
Produced at Rockfield Studios, Wales, September 1972 by Hawkwind (Dave and Del).
Highest chart place: 14 (UK)
Running time (approximately): 41:40

'Brainstorm' (Turner)

Baldly stated, the words were written while Turner was sitting on a plane waiting to go to France. He jotted down the lyrics on a notepad and came up with the music in fifteen minutes (although an early riff idea had been floating around for a little while before Turner put it all together). Julian Cope noted that all his friends thought Hawkwind were terrible because their music was so simple to play. Once punk had arrived the ability for anyone to play music was seen as a positive boon and Hawkwind were a primary inspiration. Cope, of course, has since reversed his stance and has come to see the simplicity and repetition of many Hawkwind songs as notes of genius. 'Brainstorm' is the archetypal simple musical structure, stretched by repetition to infinite lengths. Hawkwind played it for up to 20 minutes at some gigs but, theoretically, it can go on forever.

Opening with the bludgeoning 'Brainstorm' the band speed towards the end of the album like sprinters, even though the song is over eleven minutes long. The first words are: 'Standing on the runway, waiting to take off' and it is clear that the band is flying, in every sense. The lyric twists from its opening aircraft lift-off line to a perennial Hawkwind motif: the desire to remain human and not become an android. The pay-off line, however, finally embraces the idea of becoming non-human suggesting that the character would be happy to leave his body behind. Of course, the punishing eleven minutes of the relentless riff blankets everything else and most people spend more time complaining that they can't hear the words than admiring the issues brought to the surface.

This, and many other early Hawkwind songs and poems are informed and inspired by a great many science fiction/avant-garde authors of the time, but one of the influences rarely mentioned but endlessly utilised is that of Philip K Dick. His entire output, both science fiction and literary fiction, concerns the question of what it is to be human (and, by extension, what it is to be an artificial human or, indeed, a God). Dick's voice comes through clearly here and echoes around Robert Calvert's work for years to come.

'Space Is Deep' (Brock)

Decorated with science fiction themes 'Space Is Deep' is almost like a slower counterpoint to 'Brainstorm' with its busker-heavy acoustic guitar refrain and spiralling otherworldly noises. The words appear to have been adapted from the opening of Michael Moorcock's novel *The Black Corridor* in preparation for the *Space Ritual* tour although the plaintive chorus and desolate atmosphere are entirely Brock's own work. Again the full band provides a sympathetic mid-section before everything returns to the gentle acoustics that started the song in the first place. In its own quiet way, it is a beautiful song amidst the wired rock on offer.

'One Change' (Del Dettmar)

This brief echoed piano/synthesizer interlude maintains the raw, simplistic playing that characterises all early Hawkwind.

'Lord Of Light' (Brock)

The first of a satisfyingly cohesive trio of Brock songs, they encapsulate space rock for the casual listener. Here Brock starts with an endlessly descending guitar spiral that gradually turns into another riff-laden tramp through the night sky. The title is from a science fiction/fantasy novel by Roger Zelazny which combines European characters with a Buddhist/Hindu influenced world. The lyrics quickly reveal themselves to be markedly different from their apparent source material:

The elements that gather here
Upon this hill shall cast no fear
Of lines that match across the world
For travel which no man has ever heard
Moon that shines its beam so bright
Stones that measure the silvery light
Of energy that travels here
It happens on the seventh year

The references to stone circles, witchcraft, the four elements and ley-lines clearly show this is related to the Western mystical tradition rather than the melting pot hybrid that Zelazny posits. Moorcock has stated several times that Brock sometimes needs a little stimulus to kick-start his muse; in this case, it is the appropriation of a title that sets Brock on his way. While Brock's voice strains throughout at the high notes, the song fades and is then mixed directly into....

'Down Through The Night' (Brock)

The rather more laid-back acoustic guitar, swooshing electronics and echoed flute is part of a melodic swirl that uses lyrical repetition as a virtue:

Down, down and down
Down, down and down
Round, round and round

This is another surprisingly hummable tune that doesn't outstay its welcome and continues the lyrical focus on the blackness, and bleakness, of space. As the song fades, it descends into the choppy waters of....

'Time We Left This World Today' (Brock)

This chugging tale of misery and escape, repeats the curling lyric and washes around the bass-heavy sludge, conjuring an inescapable air of doomed menace before sliding into a throbbing Lemmy bass solo that characterises his input for his entire stint in the band. The band-led bridge regresses to the avant-garde experimentalism of the first album but picks itself up with a duelling bass and guitar solo intertwined that eventually returns to the initial riff in more restrained fashion. Lemmy and Brock trade chanted vocals all about the need for people to leave the planet Earth. This song seems like another snippet from a longer progressive-style suite that also comprises 'Down Through The Night', 'Space Is Deep', 'You Know You're Only Dreaming' and 'We Took The Wrong Step Years Ago'. The resultant single piece could happily occupy an entire concert.

Again the vocals are drowned by the noise, and again the music holds the feeling and intent of the lyrics even if they aren't comprehensible. Reappearing on *Palace Springs* many years later its mudslide rhythm is left intact although, inevitably, it sounds brighter and clearer than this incarnation. Often missed from the lists of great Hawkwind songs this deserves a re-evaluation because of its spot-on evocation of the atmosphere of the lyrics and the fact that it not only contains a commercial melody but also resonates with increasing frequency down the years.

'The Watcher' (Kilmister)

In radically different form Lemmy had previously recorded this (then known as 'You're Alone Now') on an album by tabla player Sam Gopal (1969's Escalator). Lemmy kept the brooding melody and downbeat outlook but changed everything else.

Displaying all the musical traits that would sustain his career, save for the speeding aggression, Lemmy opts for an ominous warning of the Big Brother state and its blanket CCTV surveillance. At the time this was almost science fiction, nowadays the song resonates as fact. While the lyrics were faddily rewritten to reference a comic book character (The Watcher, from Fantastic Four) the fuzz bass and dour chords suggest a much darker and more miserable future. In Lemmy's Big Brother world, independence is quashed and only his gruffly whispered words and acoustic guitar accompaniment are the true symbols of freedom in this totalitarian state. Only those who are quiet can get away from the constant intrusion. Both lyrically and musically, this fit the dystopian vision of the band and the final words and drawn out ending of the song sound like an elongated suicide note.

It is a perfect album closer. The 2018 re-recording by Hawkwind is a missed opportunity (as is the 1975 Motorhead version). Graced with piano, harmonica and a lackadaisical series of Eric Clapton guitar licks it lacks the quiet menace of the original and the disinterested vocal from Mr Dibs loses any hint of the subliminal aggression that the song so evidently needs.

Conclusion

Lemmy has noted in the past that he has misgivings about the recording quality of the album and, with hindsight, he has a point. The bass playing is fine, but the actual noise doesn't sound like the bass roar we have come to know and love. It seems somehow tinny. Apart from that slight technical hitch, this is an extremely accomplished album. It's worth noting that, while further forward in the mix, Turner seems to provide less sax than previously. This is a supremely satisfying album and another early pinnacle in their studio-recorded career.

The release of *Doremi Fasol Latido* heralded the new-look *Space Ritual* multimedia tour. The long-planned tour kicked off in early November and ran on into the New Year. With a clutch of new songs and an already impressive live record, the band felt it appropriate to record some shows with the intention of releasing a live album. What they heard on the tapes convinced them that the entire show deserved to be put out and the set quickly grew into a double album.

Space Ritual: Alive in Liverpool and London (United Artists, May 1973)

Personnel:
Robert Calvert: vocals, poetry
Dave Brock: vocals, guitars
Lemmy: bass guitar, vocals
Del Dettmar: synthesizer
Simon King: drums
Nik Turner: saxophone, vocals, flute
Dik Mik: audio generators, electronics
Recorded 12th and 30th December 1972 in Liverpool and London. Produced by Hawkwind and Vic Maile.
Highest chart place: 9 (UK)
Running time (approximately): 88:02

'Earth Calling' (Calvert)

This is a simple spoken vocal introduction from Calvert, with suitably strident experimental band backing, which was inspired by the BBC's World Service call sign: 'this is London Calling' although there are also echoes of the rather more disconcerting WWII Nazi broadcasts: 'this is Germany Calling'.

'Born To Go' (Brock/Calvert)

The band pile in immediately with a jet-propelled take on one of the many tracks debuting on this album. An astonishing guitar/bass riff props up a ten-minute monolith that features Brock soloing over the top and a pile-driving rhythm from King while Lemmy uses the bass to carry the riff when Brock is off soloing. The vocals are basically chanted and lyrically pretty slim; either concerning escaping from Earth or breaking out of convention and opening the human mind. It is the jackhammer gallop that catches the imagination however, the pounding repetition that pushes everything else aside.

'Down Through The Night' (Brock)

Brock continues to fire salvo after salvo of guitar soloing over the top of this previous album highlight. He sings well, and the change from studio acoustic to live electric guitar gives the song greater force and added weight. This definitely sounds less like a busking song and more like a mid-tempo rock stalwart. It charts the journey of the astronauts into space.

'The Awakening' (Calvert)

Trickling guitar and electronic squeals accompany this Calvert poem that depicts the starfarers being woken from their cocoons of stasis to prepare to make their 'First Landing On Medusa' (an alternative title for this poem).

'Lord Of Light' (Brock)

The live environment gives this song extra impetus and more immediacy. It also gives Dettmar and Dik Mik a chance to smother the song in electronic effects while Turner throws in a good deal of saxophone when Brock has finished singing.

'The Black Corridor' (Moorcock)

This coldly creepy poem is, in essence, a reading by Calvert of the first few paragraphs of Moorcock's novel of the same name. It creates an overwhelming sense of loneliness and a feeling of the utter indifference of the Universe towards human life. It places our starfarers at the outer edge of nothingness and invites them to look into the depths of space. Madness is, perhaps, the only sane response. It has much in common with the central theme of H.P. Lovecraft's entire written output but without the monstrous alien Gods of the Cthulhu Mythos.

'Space Is Deep' (Brock)

Lyrically reiterating the desolation of space this song attempts to provide a glimpse of hope in our starfarers' journey, albeit a small one. There is the possibility of a purpose, a reason, why these astronauts are on this voyage.

'Electronic No. 1' (Dettmar/Dik Mik)

Mercilessly producing atonal electronic noises to reinforce the atmosphere of vast and empty space there are times when the sounds produced bear a remarkable resemblance to the BBC Radiophonic Workshop's soundtracks for black and white era *Doctor Who*.

'Orgone Accumulator' (Brock/Calvert)

Propelled by a brutally insistent, monolithic riff and a chanted vocal this is the epitome of early Hawkwind. There is no subtlety here, but the pure raw energy propels the players into a headlong rush for the tape that, staggeringly, takes almost ten minutes...

For those unfamiliar with the word, and there are now many, an 'Orgone' is the term invented by scientist Doctor Wilhelm Reich in 1940 for a life force energy that permeates the universe. It sounds suspiciously close to 'The Force' from *Star Wars,* but it is several decades early. What is fascinating is that this is one of the few lyrics that have dated in the Hawkwind canon. By being so specific, it lacks the general approach adopted in most songs.

Wilhelm Reich claimed he had created a device to collect and concentrate this Orgone energy, which he termed the 'Orgone Box' and which he said could cure certain debilitating or deadly diseases. The Orgone Box was recommended for use by America's housewives and advertised as such. Unsurprisingly the puritanical side of America came to the forefront at this juncture. This, rather inevitably, lead to the banning and destruction of all the existing machines and even the blueprints for the device were burned. This undoubtedly explains the subsequent ostracism of Reich. Whether it was a product of the late 1960s imagination or implicit in Reich's original designs (which were recreated, as far as possible, from his original ideas rather than any surviving plans) the apparent way to collect Orgone energy was during sexual activity. His ideas were rediscovered in the late 1960s, the era of free love and mind expansion, and seem ready-made for plundering by psychedelic space rock bands.

Renamed the 'Orgone Accumulator' the song is, essentially, one long soundtrack for someone to make themselves happy but without the slow build-up and climax. This is an endless expanding middle period of rhythm and passion. These days people use similar rhythms in trance music to achieve much the same effect. The words, buried in the mix somewhat, confirm the intent of the song. This is sex music, bordering on the obscene, although curiously onanist in its message. The individual is placed within the machine and isolated from the outside world. All companionship is left outside. The stimulator, the vibrator, the accumulator is a machine that will encourage you to go blind, so the song tells us. The machine, renamed the 'Orgasmatron', is amusingly referenced in Woody Allen's film *Sleeper* (1973) and the idea was then recycled by Lemmy on the title track of Motorhead's *Orgasmatron* (1986) album, although, contrary to expectations, the lyrical thrust was very different.

In keeping with the curious flirtation with fascist imagery that pops up now and again in Hawkwind's substructure, the eventual aim of the machine is to produce a race of supermen immune to many diseases and all the stronger for it. The song now shows its true ironic colours as a warning rather than a celebration, although one suspects that the continued collection of Orgone energy would prove diverting. Weirdly the rhythmic structure of the song appears to be a clone of the experimental theme tune to *Doctor Who*. While that theme used tape loops and edits to create the stylised, and unique, rhythm, Hawkwind left it up to the group to provide the measured undertow. Nevertheless, the radical electronics and bravura experimentation of the *Doctor Who* theme, and the BBC Radiophonic Workshop who created it, don't get the recognition they deserve in their profound influence upon early Hawkwind.

'Upside Down' (Brock)

The staccato riff and jerky vocal introduce a discordant note into proceedings which, if anyone was falling asleep or in danger of becoming bored, unsettles a listener enough to pay attention again. Another new song, this has little lyrical profundity in its rather confused words, but it certainly causes the audience to examine their musical preconceptions. There is a belief that the vocals were overdubbed in the studio while the album was being mixed but, given the slightly garbled singing and the somewhat impenetrable lyrics, it seems odd that this would be the case or they would have done a better job of it.

'10 Seconds Of Forever' (Calvert)

This Calvert piece has the feeling of a launch countdown, or a fireside checklist read after Armageddon. The sense of nostalgia and regret is overwhelming. The sonic backing is much more muted and allows the words to be heard as they were intended.

'Brainstorm' (Turner)

This is the definitive version of this bludgeoning classic, and it gallops along for almost ten minutes before finally coming to a halt when the end of the (vinyl) side gets in the way. The current Collector's Edition CD/DVD package actually has an extra four minutes, but this really doesn't add anything to the track as it consists more of a free-form breakdown than a real continuation of the song itself. The title inspired the underground Brainstorm Comix, published by the Alchemy shop on Portobello Road, which was the launchpad for artist Bryan Talbot (who has since produced artwork for Hawkwind booklets and pamphlets) and had Hawkwind advertising in the first issue.

'Seven By Seven' (Brock)

Slowing proceedings down, this is a live rendition of the 'Silver Machine' b-side. The lyrical thrust is about attempting to reach enlightenment via the astral plane. Seven is a mystical number in many religions, and Brock plays on that with numerous numerological references:

> 7 signs rode on 7 stars, 7 ways to find the
> Long lost Bards

The magical undercurrents are clear for all to hear, especially when Brock sings about casting a spell 'that eternity chained'. This is not the first lyric of his to concern magic and witchcraft, and it won't be the last to feature the number seven.

'Sonic Attack' (Moorcock)

Space Ritual contains several firsts, but the greatest of these is the startling integration of seamless poetry into a rock-band context. In an album brimming with poetic talent, 'Sonic Attack' is still the undoubted highlight. In a contemptuous homage to the four-minute nuclear warning a studied, almost BBC standard, voice declaims its terrifying message with apparent gusto. The then-shocking advice that it gives (amongst other instructions it urges listeners 'to bring all bodies to orgasm simultaneously') is both comedic and bizarre and that is its great strength. It is a fist-clenched parody that goes right for the beating heart of the nuclear warning absurdity. Four minutes to build a shelter, say good-bye to loved ones, stock up with food and plunge into the vast white heat of a pointless post-holocaust life.

Of course, with Moorcock, we get less than three minutes of advice in the song before the sonic destruction hits. Adding again to the band's mythology Moorcock exchanges the nuclear threat of the age with the more rock and roll oriented idea of sonic annihilation. Naturally, from here, the band took on the persona of the sonic assassins and Moorcock's ideas laid the groundwork for the trilogy of Hawklords novels that eventually followed.

If the random sequence of squawks, bleeps, scrapes and distortion that accompanies the words can be called music then it, again, seems to illustrate the words profoundly in its use of noisemaking devices to soundtrack the end of the world through unbearable levels of sound pollution. Never before, or since, has a rock band so successfully married poetry and music into one operatic statement.

'Time We Left This World Today' (Brock)

It's not surprising that the Armageddon of 'Sonic Attack' is followed by the rather more laid back afterlife portrayed here in its loping tale of breaking away from malign influences. This was the second song edited down to fit the timings of vinyl although, as with 'Brainstorm', the original-length version doesn't add anything to the occasion.

'Master Of The Universe' (Brock/Turner)

Although Dave Anderson played on the studio version of this song, it is rendered into its definitive version here by the growly live bass of Lemmy. Whether as a result of epidemic madness, blind ego or mental and physical mutation, this is the song where the starfarers have finally achieved a form of immortality and are apparently able to wield the vast power of the universe. Unfortunately, the very nature of this reality is in question:

I am the centre of the universe
The wind of time is blowing through me
And it's all moving relative to me
It's all a figment of my mind
In this world that I've designed
I'm charged with cosmic energy
Has the world gone mad or is it me?

Untangling many of the ideas and themes propounded by this album will undoubtedly take the rest of Hawkwind's recorded career, even with their penchant for fantastical diversions.

'Welcome To The Future' (Calvert)

Concluding their epic double album with a dystopian vision of the future was only the final gambit in a breathtaking exercise of musical freedom. Coming at the end of a bruising 88-minute ride into science fiction hell this is the end as Armageddon. With a backing cooler and even less musical, the words paint a portrait of endless vistas either ripe for mining or already being corrupted.

Calvert's words on this album represent the first flowering of his own poetic vision which combined naturalistic rhythms, evocative words and psychedelic sound pictures with visions of environmental collapse, satirical science fiction and a fascistic Police state. Calvert sets out his apocalyptic prediction of things to come here. And all that in just two minutes.

Barney Bubbles again designed an elaborate giant fold-out sleeve for the album which is still one of the most impressive artefacts of the vinyl era. Alongside this, the tour programme provided another packed booklet of poetry, lyrics, pictures and prose on the continuing adventures of the Spaceship. It features lyrics for then unrecorded songs like 'Psychedelic Warlords (Disappear In Smoke)' and 'Infinity', and it explains a great deal about the whole *Space Ritual* storyline. The booklet was written by the lyricists on the album plus Barney Bubbles and Michael Moorcock.

The cover itself is a scintillatingly adept pastiche of the Art Nouveau paintings of Czech born artist Alphonse Mucha which, twisted by the undoubted flair and artistry of Barney Bubbles, created an enduring piece of design that has been revisited on frequent occasions. This vast and terrifying double album masterpiece is ballsy, visceral, brave and probably only possible due to the influence of drugs taken by both the band and their record company. This would never get a major label release now. Anyone who tells you drugs never made astonishing music should be locked in a room with this thundering ode to the joy of repetition and forced to listen at the loudest volume to this startlingly experimental work.

Seven men produced this monument to the power of the riff and edgy electronics, and they played like Mo Farah-on-steroids. Muscular, raw and decidedly primitive they nevertheless had room for 'poetry and swazzle' as Calvert modestly described his contribution. Conceptually he saw the album as the dreams of starfarers who are in a coma in deep space. In essence, he called it a space opera. Although I suspect no-one has heard opera music like this before!

Hawkwind present space as cold, icily beautiful, harsh, lonely and frequently an inspiration for madness. The trancelike extended rhythms and the sheer length of the songs accentuate the feeling of vastness while the poems and sounds that skitter and slide underneath imply a threat and terror at odds with almost any other progressive or psychedelic music of that time or any other. Much of the saxophone was mixed out of the final version of *Space Ritual* as it was out of tune or covering up the vocals which irked various band members. Turner himself admits that his playing wasn't as sharp as it could have been and still rates the album highly.

If you don't have this album, you will never like any rock music. Ever.

An absolute pinnacle for Hawkwind, live albums and the space rock genre. Awe-inspiring and gutsy.

While the band were polishing their gargantuan live opus, they were still touring relentlessly but found time to re-enter the studio for several sessions. Just before the live album's release the band recorded their long-awaited follow-up single to 'Silver Machine' and started work on Robert Calvert's satirical 'solo' project *Captain Lockheed and the Starfighters*.

'Urban Guerilla' (Brock/Calvert)

Inside the bubble of a hit single, hit albums and several sell-out tours, and mixing with revolutionary writers and artists, the band apparently didn't feel that 'Urban Guerilla' (first line: 'I'm an Urban Guerilla, I make bombs in my cellar') was particularly contentious. Its hard-hitting politics of nihilism and anarchy and the committed vocal from Calvert ensured that it wouldn't get much airplay, but it would attract the attention of the Police and the bomb squad. It certainly led to the Police raids on some of the band members that followed. In the search for a follow up single it's tempting to see 'Urban Guerilla' as the only song short enough to make the grade. Certainly, the subject matter was hardly likely to inspire either the record company or the purchasing public to get behind the song. The fact that both the songs featured on the single were 1950s rock and roll throwbacks with spurious psychedelic trappings is evidence of Hawkwind's less than wholehearted effort with the single.

Brock bemoans its demo quality recording, and few can argue with him, although the guitar and sax solos are both well-played. What cannot be argued is that the song itself is anything less than stupendous. Calvert attacks the lyrics like a Baader-Meinhof intellectual and puts in a gutsy and committed performance. Lyrically he inhabits the character impressively and his reference to 'a two-tone panther' refers to both the Black Panthers (the armed revolutionary movement associated with Malcolm X) and the White Panthers (an American-born anarchist collective centred around the Detroit band MC5 who advocated tearing down the old culture by all means at their disposal) who both spilt over briefly into the UK.

The advent of an IRA bombing campaign three weeks after the initial release of the single was both unfortunate and timely. Unfortunate, because the song would undoubtedly have been banned by radio, and timely because the badly recorded single was not selling well anyway, having staggered to only number 39 in the charts.

In order to hear the song in all its pent-up glory, the best version is the 1979 live b-side from the 'Shot Down In The Night' single that comes with a great vocal from Brock, wonderfully fluid lead guitar work from Lloyd Langton and a stalwart rhythm section. It stamps all over its clunky predecessor.

Looking back on the song now, it's surprising that this overtly political song wasn't given greater attention by the media or the public of the time. It illustrates, however, Hawkwind's approach to political material: often generalised in its aim, inhabiting a character viewpoint, the actual politics seem curiously naive and mainly summed up as anti-establishment. The politics of the individual allowed freedom within society, a stance espousing a vaguely anarchist philosophy of groups forming and dissipating as the need arises. The free festival, hippie, philosophy of the time chimes with this egalitarian belief and shows the band practising what they preached. Of course, the band then concentrate upon the pessimistic and disturbing aspects of the unfolding society they are searching for, and we hear a great raft of songs and musical detritus that shows up the dystopia it could so easily become. In our current world of suicide bombers, attacks on democracy, terrorism and fundamentalist attitudes it's no wonder the song is considered more relevant today than when it was first written.

'Brainbox Pollution' (Brock)

The b-side is a marvellously basic stomp that indulged Lemmy's undoubted rock and roll sensibilities. Edited down from its original seven and a half minutes it takes a tongue-in-cheek poke at a perennial Hawkwind subject: how sound can affect the human body. Everyone sounds like they are enjoying themselves here, and it's easy to understand why.

Captain Lockheed & The Starfighters (United Artists, April 1974)

Personnel:
Robert Calvert: vocals, percussion, actor
Paul Rudolph: guitars, bass
Lemmy: bass, guitar
Simon King: drums
Brian Eno: synthesizer, electronic effects
Del Dettmar: synthesizer
Nik Turner: saxophone
Dave Brock: guitar
Twink: funeral drum
Adrian Wagner: keyboards
Arthur Brown: vocals
The Ladbroke Grove Hermaphroditic Voice Ensemble: backing vocals
Vivian Stanshall: actor
Jim Capaldi: actor

Tom Mittledorf: actor
Richard Ealing: actor
Produced at Island Studios, Olympic Studios and Trident Studios, London and Radio Luxembourg (dialogue), March 1973-January 1974 by Roy Thomas Baker.
Running time (approximately): 42:14 (total), 28:03 (music)

While the live album and studio single appeared to cover up for a lack of new material (notwithstanding the new songs included on *Space Ritual*), there *was* a studio album recording featuring Hawkwind. *Captain Lockheed and the Starfighters* included both current (the entire band except Dik Mik) and future (Paul Rudolph) members of Hawkwind, as well as heavyweight guests such as Brian Eno, Arthur Brown, Twink (Pink Fairies) and Adrian Wagner. Robert Calvert had felt the need to stretch his own songwriting wings and struck out on his own, trying to build a solo career, but using many of the musicians he had come to know. He spent quite some time in the studio in 1973 and into 1974, contributing his circus ringmaster vocals to the Nektar concept album *Down To Earth* and working with Adrian Wagner on his *Distances Between Us* album and accompanying single as well as his own debut solo recording.

Robert Calvert had become fascinated by the extraordinary story of jet aircraft purchased by the West German Defence Ministry from the Americans in the 1960s. The planes were designed as light fighters and then re-tooled as heavy bombers, reconnaissance aircraft and, indeed, anything else that the West German government felt they required. The carnage, death and accident rates soared (unlike the aircraft itself), and the whole embarrassment was swept under the carpet. One of the extraordinary aspects of this album is that it was released before the scandal broke in the mainstream media. Engrossed by the story, which he first discovered by reading the aviation press when he was in one of his conspiratorial manic states, Robert Calvert originally wrote the album as a satirical theatre play before adding the songs to the mix. Featuring a writing contribution from Brock this is a Hawkwind concept album in all but name. Many of the songs have since become live staples in the Hawkwind repertoire.

The production emphasises a cleaner, clearer sound and less cluttered (or, perhaps, less smothering) mixing. If it had been done in the established Hawkwind style of the time, which would have beefed up the end result, one wonders what the record would have sounded like? Musically these are short and structured songs designed to drive the narrative along rather than the repetitious riffs of earlier albums. The dialogue sections actually work quite well and bear repeated listening, but it is the true story itself that will engage you.

The reissue has improved the sound quality no end and, for the first time, much of the ingrained depth of the album has finally come to the fore. Calvert often uses rock songs to explore more profound questions, and here he succeeds admirably. Calvert was intent upon studying the effects of high-pressure salesmanship and bribery by the American manufacturers. The F-104 Starfighter was an ageing jet aircraft being phased out by the USAF. Some bright spark at Lockheed, wanting to sell more planes, took the latest upgrade, the F-104G Starfighter, and apparently sold it as 'G for Germany', Calvert surmised. Equipping an old enemy with sub-standard aircraft and not providing any maintenance as part of the after-sales service ensured that a potential future combatant was neutralised. Sadly, the album has a relevance that carries on into the present day. Its revealing of the idiocy of governments has profound echoes today: the recent calls by the British Army to be given bullet-proof jackets that actually protect personnel, armoured vehicles that can withstand roadside bombs, landmine detectors that actually work and the recall of the Army's entire stock of new rifles because they didn't perform in either hot or cold weather conditions lends the album an air of contemporary relevance that is both shocking and hugely disappointing.

Although all the lyrics are printed in the accompanying libretto for the album, the track 'The Widow Song' was noticeable by its absence. Calvert had wanted German Velvet Underground alumni Nico to sing it and, when she proved unavailable, he simply left the song off the album. The only version of the song available appeared years later, in the 1980s when Calvert recorded a demo of the song for one of the *Hawkwind: Friends And Relations* albums. Produced in his preferred electronic style of the time, he persuaded his then-wife, Jill Riches, to sing on it.

Somewhat surprisingly, Calvert's debut album also inspired iconoclastic punk icon Jello Biafra to ground his political activism in painstakingly researched information. Biafra met Calvert on an American Hawkwind tour and asked him where he had got the material for the album: Calvert replied that he kept dossiers and clippings from technical journals and other legitimate sources that weren't widely circulated. He then used the information for lyrics, concepts, politics or study depending upon the information collated. Biafra immediately saw the advantages and embarked upon his own thoroughly researched diatribes.

'The Aerospaceage Inferno' (Calvert)

With a classic Lemmy bass and King drumming combination, this full-tilt opener sets out the stall of pithy rock songs to follow. Paul Rudolph plays impressive lead guitar and, for a brief spell, replaced Brock in Hawkwind. Calvert gets straight into the meat of his mockery by emphasising the vanity of the politicians being conned:

A flight of steel eagles tearing by
The ripped silk screaming of the rended sky
Flame on through sound and make time fly
What a good way to go…
What a good way to go

Calvert is aware of his lyrical talents at this point and adds in-jokes and references for the Hawkwind faithful:

Set the controls for the heart of the Earth
The silver machine is worth more than you're worth

The delight of this is that the lyrics relate directly to the on-going storyline (the aircraft's controls did cause crashes while low-level flying and the Starfighter was a pretty jet-age silver aircraft). Calvert is getting playful and serious at the same time.

'The Widow Maker' (Brock/Calvert)

This is Hawkwind in all but name. Brock wrote the music and plays the riff (which has a definite predecessor in the riff from Alice Cooper's 'School's Out') and Turner injects his trademark sax playing all over the track. Add in the pounding rhythm section (although it might be Rudolph playing the bass) and the sterling singing from Calvert, and you have a bona fide Hawkwind classic in the making. The title of the song comes from the numerous nicknames given to the notorious aircraft by the surviving pilots. Pilots also dubbed it the Flying Coffin to inspire confidence…

'The Right Stuff' (Calvert)

Although sharing a title with Tom Wolfe's seminal 1979 history of test pilots and the space programme, Calvert's song came six years earlier. It suggests the title was arrived at by coincidence rather than plagiarism (I suspect Tom Wolfe wasn't a Hawkwind fan, but I am open to persuasion if the evidence is there).

Calvert's singing is electronically manipulated to give the impression that he is in the cockpit and trying to talk while flying. It almost sounds like he has breathed in helium but it's not quite that high or ridiculous sounding. The lyrics, unsurprisingly, concern what it takes to be a great pilot. The music, again, is Hawkwind in all but name.

'The Song Of The Gremlin part one' (Arthur Brown/Calvert/Adrian Wagner)

After the plain rock music of the previous song, Calvert slows proceedings down and introduces a few left-field elements. Arthur Brown (admired by, and an infrequent collaborator with, Hawkwind and known for his hit single 'Fire') adds his multi-octave range to this half-spoken/half-sung declamatory keyboard and synthesizer-based track. Calvert was working on Adrian Wagner's *Distances Between Us* album around the same time, and Wagner returned the favour by co-writing the music and playing on this track. It chronicles the myth of the 'gremlin' in aviation history and, by implication, the astonishingly poor maintenance record of the F-104G Starfighters. There are tales of the engine literally falling out of a Starfighter in mid-air.

'Hero With A Wing' (Calvert)

Here Calvert praises the bravery and courage of the pilots assigned to fly these death trap machines. In a first-person narrative, Calvert relates the tale of a flying ace doomed from take-off. The dirge-like pace, electronic effects and rattling percussion give a sense of the rickety nature of the whole enterprise.

'Ejection' (Calvert)

There is a contemporaneous Hawkwind version of this song that adds a crackling dive bomber opening but is otherwise pretty similar to the album version here. A rollicking rock song, this plunges headlong into Hawkwind territory and, needless to say, has been a regular live favourite for the band. It ends with the sound of a crashing Starfighter and, in the meantime, concerns a pilot realising that ejecting from his plane is the only sensible option. Unfortunately, an early manufacturing fault meant that a lot of the ejector seats didn't actually work, either punching the pilot through the canopy or not ejecting the pilot at all. Both would prove fatal.

'The Song Of The Gremlin part two' (Brown/Calvert/Wagner)

Returning to the gremlins; the initial free-jazz saxophone, clattering percussion and shouted vocals give way to a further dirge-like pace and a briefly sung chorus which is repeated and then fades out on the opening musical chaos. There is a feeling of hopelessness and resignation to the words that match the avant-garde backing, making it both powerful and uncomfortable.

'Catch A Falling Starfighter' (Calvert)

To end this satirical ode to death and destruction, there is a slow funeral march which uses a folk drum beat while Calvert sings a hymn-like lament to the fatally flawed aircraft. The clear implication is that Calvert is spearing the vanity and insanity of the political class and their greed. To date there have been 292 Starfighter crashes, claiming the lives of 115 pilots. The vast majority of these were West German in origin.

What Happened Next

Del Dettmar's desire to emigrate to Canada and play something quieter lead to the band contacting ex-High Tide and Third Ear Band violinist Simon House. As well as doubling up on keyboards Simon was well-known to the band and, they felt, would fit right in. He joined around February of 1974. The band made their second jaunt into America under the umbrella of the 1999 Party, adding new songs to the set and changing the *Space Ritual* set-up of only a few months before. While they had produced a marvellous stage show the band were already keen to be moving on.

Hall of the Mountain Grill (United Artists, September 1974)

Personnel:
Dave Brock: lead guitar, 12 string guitar, synthesizers, organ, vocals
Lemmy: bass, guitars, vocals
Simon King: drums, percussion
Simon House: keyboards, synthesizer, violin
Del Dettmar: keyboards, synthesizer, kalimba
Nik Turner: saxophone, oboe, flute, vocals
Recorded January 1974 (live), May 1974 (studio)
Produced at Olympic Studios, London by Hawkwind and Doug Bennett, May-June 1974. Live songs produced by Roy Thomas Baker, January 1974.
Highest chart place: 16 (UK)
Running time (approximately): 41:37

'The Psychedelic Warlords (Disappear In Smoke)' (Brock)

The angry buzzing that fades in at the beginning of the album mirrors the angry buzzing of the lyrics. In a rare outing into politics the album starts in a melodically mid-tempo rage:

> Sick of politicians
> Harassment and laws
> All we do is get screwed up
> By other people's flaws

The choppy guitar and bass throb lend weight to a lyrical attack on the 'modern' urban world and the venal and greedy people who create ever more restrictive boundaries for civilization. There are some lovely unobtrusive production touches which polish up the songs a notch or two but still leave room for blurting saxophone and tuneful but ragged vocals. The lyrics, with two ultimately unused verses at the beginning, were first seen in the *Space Ritual* tour programme. Following the revolutionary politics of 'Urban Guerilla' with this militant harangue of the status quo was a bold move by the band. Hammering home their unavoidably political stance the song quickly becomes both more melodic in its approach and increasingly whingeing in its lyrical tone. The song has the curious effect of seeming slower in real life than it is in the memory. For some reason, we hear this song faster than its almost funereal pace. It's an odd phenomenon. The fade-out is an impressive mix of wah-wah guitar, stuttered vocals, pounding bass and steam train cymbals that wash into the next track seamlessly.

'Wind Of Change' (Brock)

The increasing musicality and complexity of the band's music is reflected in the trio of instrumentals that litter this album. The first sounds highly progressive (and even classical) in its arrangement and is remarkable in its prominent use of the violin and mellotron skills of Simon House. Much use is made of the wind effect before the organ and mellotron insinuate themselves into the neo-classical proceedings, and then a beautiful violin solo skims over the top like a gull flying over waves. Here, perhaps, is the first sign that Brock was also looking to create soundtrack music for films or television, although it ultimately came to very little.

The title phrase comes from a 1960 speech in the South African parliament by British Prime Minister Harold Macmillan regarding 'the wind of change blowing through the continent' (Africa, presumably) although it would be decades before revolution, rebellion and the downfall of apartheid would occur. In the meantime, we are left with this surprisingly sophisticated and melodic tune belying the dark undercurrents of the title.

'D-Rider' (Turner)

A rather cack-handed guitar riff opens this 'everything and the kitchen sink' production. Lemmy tries a new form of bass-playing that consists of heavy noodling and the vocals are covered in effects (echoing, phasing) while the mellotron does its unique synthesised chorale party trick. Turner's vocals are buried in the mix at times, and he seems to have had an off day when he was recording his contributions as the singing is disinterested until the semi-chorus kicks in and the saxophone playing is light on tunefulness, lacking in depth and mercifully brief. While by no means dreadful, this is the first hint that Hawkwind aren't bullet-proof and it is the fussiness and multi-layered nature of the song that hampers it.

The song is also known as 'Dragon Rider' which suggests that it was inspired by Anne McCaffrey's fantasy epic about the planet Pern and its' human/dragon partnerships.

'Web Weaver' (Brock)

Brock's muse is on open display here; regardless of the words, this sounds like a psychedelic love song with its melodic guitar soloing, busking 12 string guitar and piano blending with the airy voice of Brock soaring over the top. Brock seems to be singing, again, about the effects that music can have on us all, this time concentrating upon the less desirable elements:

> Larynx cries no longer heard
> A chord was struck that chilled the nerve

There is a dichotomy here when the band then stretch out into a delightful instrumental break which again highlights the greater musicianship and melody on offer whilst completely negating the lyrical thrust of the song.

'You'd Better Believe It' (Brock)

Beginning the old 'side two' of an LP, this is like a carbon copy opening of 'side one' (with its synthesizer drone) but at a faster pace. Bolting an almost folk-fiddle violin to the undercarriage of a sprightly rock song is addictive and, adding in the brand new squidgy synthesizer sound, this has a distinctly 1970s grandeur to it. This is particularly due to the cosmic verses and down-to-earth chorus which juxtapose each other so nicely. In a vocal parallel to their already impressive musical telepathy Brock and Lemmy trade vocals on the chorus like brothers. Lemmy also provides distinctive backing and harmony vocals throughout the album. This is one of three songs recorded live that were comprehensively over-dubbed in the studio and sound considerably different in their original live incarnations. For some reason, this song didn't last very long in the live arena but it deserves a reappraisal and could slip quite easily into a nostalgia-heavy setlist of rarities.

'Hall Of The Mountain Grill' (Simon House)

The beautiful neo-classical piano harmonics of House's title track are rich and artfully played. It doesn't have any hint of the debased phrase 'ambient' about it and it is over far too quickly, fading out just when a further movement or extrapolation seems imminent. Given the instrumentation, this seems to be an entirely solo piece by House. Obliquely referencing Edvard Grieg's 'In The Hall Of The Mountain King' the sleeve notes give the game away of the title with the 'Legend of Beenzon Toste' which mythologises the bands oft-frequented Ladbroke Grove café and commemorates it with a short piece of rhyming verse (probably from the pen of Nik Turner, although no-one has laid claim to it).

'Lost Johnny' (Mick Farren/Kilmister)

Although a musical nod back to Lemmy's rock'n'roll roots this has Mick Farren (of the Deviants) writing disquieting words to a spirited bass-heavy tune. As a song, it stands out from its album counterparts because it is so very straight in comparison. It is clear that Lemmy played the guitar parts himself here, mostly because (as Lemmy often said) he really wasn't a great guitarist. The basic lead guitar work is notable as workmanlike but nothing else and the solo is perfunctory but serviceable. Farren, however, throws in a mish-mash of ideas lyrically (werewolves, crocodiles living in the sewers of New York, characters named Sally and Simon, and mentions of morphine, tuinol and valium) but fails to tie the song together with a single theme or statement.

'Goat Willow' (Dettmar)

This is another remarkable instrumental that has classical leanings, especially as it utilises orchestral instruments including harpsichord and flute, while simultaneously using all the keyboards and synthesizers at the band's disposal. This is what spaced out music for Henry VIII would sound like.

Goat willow is also known as pussy willow or great sallow. Just so you know.

'Paradox' (Brock)

Hawkwind are renowned (and, occasionally, reviled) for re-recording old songs in different arrangements. While not musically cribbed from an earlier song, the recycling starts here with lyrics snatched from 'Down Through The Night' and 'Seeing It As You Really Are' blended together. As a final song, it reintroduces the psychedelic rock bent of the album but overlays it with the piano and mellotron so prevalent elsewhere. Again based on an initial live recording it's hard to imagine what the original sounded like without the blanket of overdubs. Lemmy and Brock sing marvellous harmonies here, the lightness of Brock's voice, complemented by the alcohol and cigarettes rasp of Lemmy.

'It's So Easy' (Brock)

Three songs slated for this album were recorded in concert with Roy Thomas Baker (most well known for his 1970s work with Queen) producing. Captured one night at Edmonton Sundown this is the b-side that never made it to the final album selection. It has all the classic 1973 Hawkwind trademarks (plodding pace, a sterling Brock vocal, a simple chorus, thumping drums and low down bass) but it doesn't prepare the audience for the change of sound that House provided with the overpowering mellotron and keyboard overdubs that weren't apparent on the day of the live recording. Audience members who had attended and then bought the album and single months later must have wondered if their memories were faulty. Regardless, this is a pleasing tramp of a song that deserves its place on the remastered album as a more fitting end than 'Paradox'.

Conclusion

The album sessions were marked by their easygoing nature and the considerable experimentation that went on between the musicians. This is a startlingly mature album from a group characterised as drug casualties. It is wonderful, and with a longevity that belies its origins.

Perhaps one of the least likely bands to be influenced by Hawkwind is Roxy Music. Their 1972 debut album begins with a four-minute encapsulation of Hawkwind in the form of 'Re-make/Re-model'. By November 1974's *Country Life* the band were still using various Hawkwind ideas; none more so than on 'Out Of The Blue' where Roxy Music distil *Hall Of The Mountain Grill*, complete with electric violin, sturdy bass, ambient saxophone, psychedelic backwards guitars, phasing and more, into a single 4 and a half minute song. Musically this is like a lost Hawkwind classic.

At the end of the album sessions, King managed to break a few ribs playing football in a bands and roadies league. As he was only going to be out of action for a few weeks, the band didn't see the need to recruit a permanent replacement so, for a short series of European dates in June of 1974, they recruited seasoned session drummer Alan Powell. By the time gigging resumed in August King was well enough to play again and, in a curious move, the band decided to retain Powell as well, thus ushering in the twin drummer period or, as Lemmy dubbed them, the 'drum empire'. The fallout from this decision would lead to a dramatic change in the band and its fortunes only one album later.

Warrior On The Edge Of Time (United Artists, May 1975)

Personnel:
Dave Brock: vocals, guitars, bass guitar, synthesizers
Simon House: keyboards, synthesizers, violin
Lemmy: bass guitar
Simon King: drums, percussion
Alan Powell: drums, percussion
Nik Turner: saxophone, vocals, flute
Michael Moorcock: vocals
Produced at Rockfield Studios, Monmouth by Hawkwind, February-March 1975.
Highest chart place: 13 (UK)
Running time (approximately): 46:05

'Assault And Battery part 1' (Brock)

Opening with this extraordinary one-two punch sets out the grand stall for the album. While Brock undoubtedly wrote the music, one of the crowning glories is the adroit bass-line that Lemmy opens the album with. It drives the song and provides a momentum that would be sorely lacking with almost any other bass player. The odd mellotron backing to the rhythm is interrupted by a brief flute, and then the vocals kick in with the uplifting joy of the song revealed. Although the production is somewhat rougher, and the songwriting is not as complex, this is where Hawkwind's adoption into the progressive rock fraternity is truly cemented. They may not be Yes or Genesis, but they have their own intricacies and they are unafraid to stretch out and create song suites that run the gamut from bass-heavy rock to quasi-classical opera without losing any of the inherent identity of Hawkwind. This, ultimately, storms along like a steam locomotive. The memorable opening stanzas for this song:

> Lives of great men all remind us
> We may make our lives sublime
> And departing leave behind us
> Footprints in the sands of time

actually come from 'The Psalm Of Life' by American poet Henry Wadsworth Longfellow (1807-1882) which Brock cheekily appropriated and then provided a further verse and a chorus to complete the song. These four poetic lines recur in a number of Hawkwind and Brock tunes that follow. Brock was deeply into fantasy fiction and mythology at this time and finds himself singing about Stonehenge (or, perhaps, another Neolithic stone circle site):

> Of hewn stones the sacred circle
> Where the wizened sages sat

This is clearly one of the 'footprints' that has inspired Brock to pen the song in the first place and his appropriation of the initial lines is akin to his requests to Moorcock for a concept which he then mutates into his own songs or themes for an album. As the words are then repeated, it is clear that Brock felt his point had been made without the need for further lyrical invention. The rush of the music survives a flute and swirling organ-driven middle eight before the repetition of the lyrics leads to a slowing of the pace and a phenomenal segue into...

'The Golden Void part 2' (Brock)

Heralded by a gong strike and then a brain-searing violin note stretched to breaking point, this is anything but an ambient comedown attempt. Brock's light vocal hangs over a mid-tempo rock song of harmonic appeal which features a fine sax performance from Turner and a great deal of distended notes from either the electric guitar or the violin bubbling under in the mix. Lyrically this is the only song to reference the 'concept' that had been drawn up by Moorcock, and it doesn't really explain the idea or provide any hint of a storyline in progress, although it does bring the album title into its chorus which is a bonus. As with many Hawkwind songs, however, it is the music that carries the day, and this is a definite case in point, even if the lyrics are nicely worded and musically in context.

'The Wizard Blew His Horn' (Moorcock/House/Simon King/Alan Powell)

Rather bellicose in his delivery of the cribbed imagery, Moorcock is left to fend for himself as the 'music' is little more than cymbal washes and synthesised soundscapes. Layering on vocal effects over the declamatory tone adds nothing to the piece but makes the whole two minutes more of an ordeal for the listener. Moorcock has a few memorable lines and phrases here but invests the whole thing with so much overblown histrionics that the effect becomes noise without meaning.

'Opa-Loka' (King/Powell)

Powered by a highly Neu! influenced motorik beat, this is the sound of two drummers adding up to less than the sum of one drummer. Lemmy was, reportedly, so pissed off with the drum empire that he slept through the recording of this tune and it is Brock who appears on bass here. As a gently looping instrumental this deserved to be a forgotten b-side to an obscure single, not given a prime place on the album.

Alan Powell had previously lived in the town of Opa-Locka in Florida, hence the name. As the track begins to fade and the synthesizers and sound effects take over it is finally time for:

'The Demented Man' (Brock)

This is the last gasp of Brock's busking heritage, and it rather sounds like it. Pretty guitar chords and the floating folk-tinged voice mix with the crying gull calls and synthesised wind noises to produce the slightest of Brock's acoustic tunes. The words are confused (or, if we are feeling generous, deep but somewhat impenetrable) although the general tone is downbeat and appears to be concerned with regret and powerlessness. The repeated phrase 'which way I'll go' is the nearest the song gets to a chorus and there's a distinct chance that anyone busking this song will go home with even emptier pockets than when they started, such is its dour outlook.

'Magnu' (Brock)

Starting with the same synthesised wind effect this quickly develops into an album highlight by virtue of its sterling violin soloing, sawing guitar riff, full-blooded effects-laden Brock vocal, inventive bass work, surprising hand drum/bongo accompaniment, seamless sax fills and pounding rhythm. All this could sound cluttered, but instead, it is gloriously indulgent. The words are mostly by Brock but are heavily under the influence of arch-Romantic radical poet Percy Bysshe Shelley (1792-1822) and contain phrases and ideas from his original poem 'Hymn to Apollo'. As 'Magnu' finally fades out, on what can only be described as a stuttering Dalek vocal, the wind effect returns and the next recitation begins.

'Standing At The Edge' (Moorcock/House/King/Powell)

Nik Turner gives this his all but it suffers from the same disappointing backing (this time it's clunking bells, synthesizer swoops and kettle drums) and the same portentous vocals overlaid with effects (echo, ring modulator and what we would now know as mobile phone breakup) that hamstring the three poetry readings presented here. Some of the words are bastardised from 'Sonic Attack', and this reinforces the derivative nature of these poems. Moorcock seems to be parodying himself at times. Coining the phrase 'Veteran of a Thousand Psychic Wars' in this piece, Moorcock presented a set of lyrics to Eric Bloom of Blue Oyster Cult six years later and was rewarded with a stirring and martial musical arrangement for his emotive and powerful vision of the traumatic effects of war. The disappointment is that the original words here are all bluster and startling imagery but lack any meaningful theme by comparison.

'Spiral Galaxy 28948' (House)

House delivers the second instrumental to surface here but, unlike 'Opa-Loka', it has a strong melody, a memorable tune and some new sounds to show off. Beginning with burly synthesised chords and a plodding rhythm it heads off at a sprightly tempo once a simple guitar strum is introduced and then flies off into space with, essentially, a muddied up keyboard solo carrying on through to the end, occasionally making way for flute and guitar interference on the way. Although it looks like galactic coordinates the '28948' is, in fact, House's date of birth.

'Warriors' (Moorcock/House/King/Powell)

This is where Moorcock's voice is put through a ring modulator and sounds like an effete Dalek. The entry gong makes its reappearance before Moorcock starts speaking and then the percussive backing intrudes, adding random keyboard/synthesizer elements to the buzzing voice shouting about death and destruction. The one thing that separates this from its forebears on the album is the astonishing imagery and clever use of words on display here. All of his contributions are drawn from Moorcock's own Eternal Champion mythology and, here, there is a hint that there was a plan for the album. Instead, we had to wait a decade until *The Chronicle of the Black Sword* would see the fruition of a full Moorcock concept taken to its conclusion.

'Dying Seas' (Turner)

Brock suggests the demo version of this song is the one used on the album and this is hard to refute. It's a thick, muddy soup of a song that gives the impression that it is slowing down and somewhat out-of-tune except for the violin and keyboard parts. Turner spends some time blaring his sax in a distinctly non-musical manner and slurring his singing as if he has smoked too much dope and the whole enterprise seems flat and misguided. Lyrically indistinct, only the title suggests an environmental concern at the state of the oceans.

'Kings Of Speed' (Brock/Moorcock)

This song was originally written for Moorcock's only album to date. Brock liked the song, cannibalised it by twisting the music and rewording it, and then gave it to the band. Lemmy, apparently, loved it, being the king of Speed himself. As a basic rock and roll riff powers up it's only the keyboard embellishments that mark it out as Hawkwind. Lyrically this is not complicated or literary. They do refer to further Moorcock characters, this time from his Jerry Cornelius novels, like 'Mr C' himself and 'Frank [Cornelius, Jerry's brother] and [Bishop] Beasley's rocket ship' but the tone is playful and the words appear to be an end-of-recording-sessions addition. The original Moorcock demo is fascinating for how different it is in both song and execution. The words are almost entirely unrecognisable, except for the title, and the music is blandly formulaic.

The Hawkwind version is also formulaic but in a very extroverted way. Given the subject matter, this seems rather more appropriate than the pedestrian Moorcock demo.

'Motorhead' (Kilmister)

While the band were busy recording the album and guesting on solo albums by Moorcock and Calvert, a single b-side containing Lemmy's final writing contribution to the band was released. Coupled with 'Kings of Speed', Lemmy produced an equally scuzzy counterpart called 'Motorhead'. Delighting in the fact that this is the only rock and roll song to feature the word 'parallelogram' Lemmy gave Hawkwind a parting gift of surprising weight. There are two versions available: the first contains a vocal by Dave Brock (which sounds odd when you initially hear it) and has a guitar solo, while the second version (released on the single) has the familiar Lemmy growl but replaces the guitar with a violin solo. Undoubtedly strange to hear a violin part on the song but it works extremely well and Lemmy was not backwards in his praise for House's musicianship, commitment and defiantly rock stance.

Conclusion

Rather than a simple gatefold, the original LP folded out into a stunning Chaos shield design. Obviously inspired by Barney Bubbles previous sleeves in its intricacies, this album very definitely took a sword-and-sorcery route rather than the science fiction of yesteryear. Proper shield covers are now extremely hard to find and the CD reissues have found it impossible to reproduce it.

Critical opinion has been harsher than fan opinion to this album. The dichotomy of views is startling. Fans acknowledge this as a masterpiece, critics (and Lemmy) are much less enamoured of this psychedelic fantasy trip. Given the confusing and rambling nature of this beast of an album, it's easy to see why sides have been taken. For every storming bass-led rock song, like 'Assault And Battery' and 'Magnu', there are directionless rhythmic drum workouts like 'Opa-Loka' or lame busking songs like 'The Demented Man'.

It is worth noting, however, that Turner's playing on this album is much more structured, increasingly melodic and far better played than on previous outings. In addition, it gains some prominence in the mix on occasions where this can be heard. It is a pity, then, that his songwriting prowess seems to have deserted him at this time. In common with the previous album though, the album possesses an eerily beautiful instrumental, 'Spiral Galaxy 28948', and a marvellous neo-classical piece, 'The Golden Void part two', which soars with House's searing violin to the fore. By the time the turgid 'Dying Seas' appears, the album has gone into decline and its only rescue is from the breathless but basic rock and roll of 'Kings Of Speed'. The lack of Dettmar's oscillator intrusions (he left the band before the album sessions had begun) is hardly noticeable as the band sweep through the album.

It is Simon House and his musicianship that saves this album from the bargain bins. His playing is inventive and charismatic, while many of the spoken pieces are not. In an album of patchy thirds (one-third disappointing, one-third reasonable and one-third great) there are simply too many lows to place it at the top of the list. The advent of the 2013 remaster/remix has made the album almost indispensable, however.

With the recording sessions for *Warrior On The Edge Of Time* and Moorcock's *The New World's Fair* albums finished in March and the sessions for Calvert's second solo, *Lucky Leif and the Longships*, winding up in April the band, as ever, went out on tour. The same month that *Warrior On The Edge Of Time* was released, Lemmy, in a rare joint band decision, was fired after a drugs bust on the Canadian border. According to all the band members, this was not simply due to this single incident, but in relation to his erratic and wayward behaviour. Lateness and a completely different routine didn't endear him to his bandmates and his continuing problems with the twin drummer line-up meant that the drug arrest gave the band an excuse to dump their iconic bass player. Brock actually invited Lemmy back into the group within days, but band opinion was against him, and the return never happened. This single piece of information should give the lie to the oft-repeated belief that Hawkwind is purely Brock's band.

Whichever way you look at it the band were never the same again. Whether through quirk of circumstance or fate, the band simultaneously lost their recording contract and the bedrock of their live show. Paul Rudolph, accomplished musician and ex-member of The Deviants and the Pink Fairies, was flown across the Atlantic at a moment's notice and carried on the tour to its scheduled end.

3: Charisma and Quarks (1976-1979)

The arrival of Paul Rudolph seems to have provoked a crisis of confidence in Brock. Naturally a lead or rhythm guitar player rather than a bassist, Rudolph began to swap instruments with Brock at gigs and on recordings. Unsure of his own playing ability at the time, Brock could clearly see that Rudolph had an edge. In addition, Alan Powell felt he had an onstage accomplice who could play in the more advanced, intricate and dynamic way that he was looking for. It was to usher in the first signs of complete disintegration that were to thwart the band's career.

This was the moment at which Calvert re-entered the scene. At the Reading Festival in August 1975, he joined the band on stage to read new poetry, sing and provide percussion. Almost immediately he rejoined the band full-time; partly as a response to his already surprisingly moribund solo career and partly to work on the increasingly theatrical stage presence he wanted to explore, and the band were a perfect vehicle for that. The day after the same Festival appearance another mainstay of the band decided to move on. Having spent four years on the road with an all-male band, Stacia had finally called it a day. She left to get married, and the band lost another key draw. Signing to Charisma Records (home of Lindisfarne, Genesis and Van Der Graaf Generator among others) the band began work on their first post-Lemmy album.

In July 1976, another Hawkwind related object was released: *The Time of the Hawklords* (predating the band name switch by two years), purporting to be by Moorcock and Michael Butterworth but actually written entirely by Butterworth, was a science fiction novel featuring the entire line-up of Hawkwind (in the guise of their fictional stage personas) as the main protagonists fighting against the Death Generator in a post-apocalyptic London with their music as weapons. The band were given somewhat penetrable, pseudonyms (Baron Brock, Count Motorhead, The Thunder Rider, etc.,) while the prose bounded along as a series of overblown set pieces tied together with pulp plotting and seemingly amphetamine-fuelled rhythmic composition. It isn't always easy to read, but its basic tale of rock music vs pop music (I imagine the Death Generator is destroying the world using The Carpenters or Abba as its primary weapon) is certainly a lot of fun, and the in-jokes and references are a real bonus. The first part of a projected trilogy (the sales were modest but deemed sufficient for a second book to be commissioned), Moorcock claims that his only involvement was writing the first paragraph and providing the briefest of outlines for the first novel. While the band were featured in the narrative they had no input into it and could concentrate on the next album.

Astounding Sounds, Amazing Music (Charisma, August 1976)

Personnel:
Dave Brock: vocals, guitars, synthesizers
Robert Calvert: vocals, percussion

Nik Turner: vocals, saxophone, flute
Simon King: drums, percussion
Simon House: violin, keyboards
Alan Powell: drums, percussion
Paul Rudolph: bass guitar, keyboards
Dave Gilmour: acoustic guitar
Produced at Roundhouse Studios, London by Hawkwind, February-April 1976.
Highest chart place: 33 (UK)
Running time (approximately): 38:31

'Reefer Madness' (Brock/Calvert)

Perhaps in order not to frighten away long-time listeners, the album begins with the two most traditional riff-heavy and lengthy beasts before it diversifies. It is immediately noticeable that the production is clearer, cleaner, less slapdash and more song-focused. For some reason, we start with the sound of a train whistling past and, in the middle, we get the sound of an aircraft taking off. What this has to do with the satirical subject matter of the song is anybody's guess. The title comes from a dreadfully earnest 1936 Christian-funded American propaganda film which proves unintentionally hilarious as it is so poorly acted, highly sensationalised and utterly preposterous. It is supposed to warn parents of the dangers of marijuana use but was almost immediately taken up by the exploitation film circuit and re-edited to accentuate the more sensational elements.

Calvert presents the case for the prosecution, albeit firmly tongue-in-cheek, in the early verses and then, after a squealing and chaotic instrumental section, spins a hallucinatory tale of cannabis consequences:

> One night I was smoking dope
> When I looked at my hands and I saw
> I had eleven fingers
> One of these fingers fell from my hand
> Onto the carpet
> Crawled across the floor, up on my shelf
> Inside my piggy bank and stole my stash!

Clearly a parody, Calvert illustrates his emerging lyrical ability with aplomb.

'Steppenwolf' (Brock/Calvert)

The origins of this song are clear: Brock played Calvert a sinuous riff that he had come up with and Calvert immediately thought some lyrics he had previously written for Adrian Wagner's keyboard-smothered 1974 *Distances Between Us* album would fit. Retaining the vocal melody from the 1974 original and placing it in a rock context, courtesy of the scything guitar, Brock and Calvert stretched the song out to highlight Simon House's violin and keyboard skills in the instrumental sections and Calvert's extra verses. Turner provides restrained saxophone, and the rhythm section merge in with precision. Lyrically inspired by Herman Hesse's novel of the same name (and not by the similarly named 1960s 'Born To Be Wild' band) it is a study of the breakdown of urban life, from the detached viewpoint of a writer in his garret imagining he is a werewolf on the hunt in the city at night and the theatricality of his lyrics were not lost on Calvert who took to prowling the stage in a frock coat and top hat. Brock's loping music is perfectly wound around Calvert's words and primal vocalising, and the whole song passes much too quickly.

'City Of Lagoons' (Powell)

The first of the instrumentals that litter this album is a jazz-funk piece, unsurprisingly driven by its drumming, that lays a down a slow groove that could, theoretically, carry on for hours. The unadorned bluesy electric guitar notes border on reggae and easy listening, clearly Rudolph in a relaxed mood, while the synthesizer sounds are undoubtedly Pink Floyd or Krautrock inspired. Swirling comfortably to a fade the track is melodic without being intrusive.

'The Aubergine That Ate Rangoon' (Paul Rudolph)

This is the most startling song on the album comprising, as it does, of pure instrumental funk with backwards wordless vocals rising like shadows from the mix. The bass and synthesizer work have more in common with Parliament or Funkadelic of the time and both this and the preceding track are noticeable for Brock's entire absence from proceedings. The musical direction explored here is simply a one-off, although it has its merits as a striking and innovative piece of music for Hawkwind to release.

'Kerb Crawler' (Brock/Calvert)

Possessing a Lemmy-friendly rock and roll riff, this feels like a throwback after the sonic excursions of the instrumentals. Calvert starts by praising the car he is cruising the streets with and then proceeds to lard on the sleaziness of the situation with comments about 'high heels clicking' and German red-light districts before mercifully coming to a close. A lyric about picking up prostitutes was never going to be very commercial, particularly as the vocals are so blatant and high in the mix. Released as a re-mixed single, it has all the hallmarks of desperation about it: prominent female backing singers singing the title, bouncing rhythm, brass accompaniment, prurient lyrics and a re-mix by a big name, in this case, David Gilmour of Pink Floyd. Less than the sum of its parts this is a blot on the album and on the Hawkwind name, although it does seem like a product of its time lyrically. Particularly from the traditional American viewpoint, Ry Cooder has always insisted that the only things you should sing about are 'cars and girls'. Calvert managed a two-in-one on this occasion.

'Kadu Flyer' (House/Turner)

Embracing that synthesised wind effect again, this has a perky piano opening and fits right in with the instrumental pieces musically while Turner sings of breaking free and flying away (possibly from the increasingly bitter rows that were a feature of the band at the time) 'higher and higher' into new vistas as the protagonist tries to glide over Mount Everest. Perhaps these lyrics were unconscious but they were prescient as Turner would be far out of the band by the end of 1976 and recording flute improvisations inside the King's Chamber of the Great Pyramid of Cheops in Egypt. Far out, indeed.

The lyrics were originally credited to Jamie Mandelkau (former Pink Fairies manager and a friend of Turner's who later became an author) as Turner was in contention with either the record company or manager Doug Smith (it remains unclear) at the time and this was a legal loophole that Brock had previously used successfully on 'Silver Machine'.

'Kadu' is a shortened version of Kathmandu which formed part of the 1960s hippie trail that went through India and Nepal and probably accounts for the Eastern-sounding saxophone and the de rigueur use of Indian instruments in the long tail section and fade-out. What sounds like a backwards gong strike ends the song in a strange style.

'Chronoglide Skyway' (House)

The wind effect returns, briefly, and then House conjures another breathtaking instrumental from his colleagues, complete with another bluesy guitar solo from Rudolph, providing a fine lift for the end of the album proper. As with all of House's compositions, this is both melodically rich and musically intricate. It highlights the essential dichotomy of the album, however, as it fits well into the smoother stream of instrumentals and 'Kadu Flyer' but sits uneasily with the cleaner rock-driven sound of the few Brock-fuelled songs.

'Honky Dorky' (Brock/Calvert/House/King/Powell/Rudolph/Turner)

This was the Dave Gilmour-mixed b-side to 'Kerb Crawler' and seems like a genuine find. Until that is, you realise the piece is simply an elongated extract from the instrumental middle section of the rambunctious 'Reefer Madness'! Delicately remixed and subtly overdubbed it may be, but this is recycling as it's never been heard before. It also suggests that the band had little time for single releases and made use of anything to hand for the b-side.

'Time For Sale' (Calvert/Rudolph)

This funk-driven epic was only ever played on the supporting tour for the album and is only available in a poorly recorded live version, but it is a little gem that would have sat on the album itself with ease. It has a curling funk bass and uncharacteristic, almost rapped, verse vocals before the chorus kicks in with typical Hawkwind style although the key change midway through is extremely unusual and adds a great deal to the quirky progression. Yes, I did say 'rapped'; if you listen to this song, I can't think how else to describe the singing here. It is certainly before its' time. Brock adds nice back-up vocals on the more traditional chorus and Calvert sings at his best almost throughout. The lyrics are, perhaps, a little rough (concerning, as they appear to do, the selling of time although there are apparently unrelated mentions of Helen of Troy) but Calvert puts his all into the breathy late section which again raises the bar for this song. Such a shame there isn't a studio-recorded version as there are times when the live source is evident with its electric crackles and lack of guitar and saxophone in the mix. It is worth hunting out, even in this form. Although initially credited to Brock/Calvert there is clearly no denying this is Rudolph's writing, and the credits here are undoubtedly accurate. This live track was recorded on 27 September 1976 at the Colston Hall in Bristol.

'The Dream of Isis' (Brock/House/King)

Although recorded a couple of months after the album's release, and featuring a reduced line-up (Turner and Powell were absent), this is a lovely instrumental that is an actual rarity. Even today this piece only appears on compilations, and that's rather a shame as it is well worth owning. Featuring a front-and-centre bass line, a scraping and repetitious synthesizer sound, wordless vocals and a quirky drum pattern this deserves a place on its parent album as it suits the dope-suffused atmosphere very well. The song is probably named after the ancient Egyptian goddess of fertility, but there is also the possibility that it draws from the alternative name given to the river Thames as it passes through Oxford.

'Back On The Streets' (Calvert/Rudolph)

The raucous 'Back On The Streets' single emphatically doesn't deserve a place on the album though. This is more punk than pot and doesn't really gel with anything until the live Hawklords experience; using the same initial guitar riff and coming from the same musical place as 'Kerb Crawler' it sits uneasily with the musical smorgasbord being recorded at the time. This startlingly punky song served to realign the band with the current musical flavour, and it still sounds very punky today, and that effect is only enhanced by Calvert's idiosyncratic vocal. Produced by outside man Bob Potter (largely known for producing Paul Kossoff's projects) it would have made a decent double A-side with 'Kerb Crawler' but adds nothing new to the basic rock and roll on offer. Unrepresentative of the album it followed, and preceded, it was, nevertheless, played on the tour for the album and gained both a sterling middle verse:

Joules of sound are bad for your hearing
And pleasure's something that doesn't last
I took a substance for disappearing
And I faded in the mirror so fast

... and a rousing fiddle break which was the best part of the song. The writing credit for Rudolph is curious as this sounds very much like a patent Brock riff and progression although no-one has challenged the writing credits for this. Perhaps the two were a little more simpatico than was first realised.

'Where Are They Now?' (Brock)

An otherwise unreleased song from the album sessions that was dusted off for a Weird Tapes release in the 1980s, this is a plaintive Brock piece that would have suited the album. It was tried again in 2013 and released on the Spacehawks compilation/sampler of re-recordings and still sounded commercial but intrinsically Hawkwind in flavour. The title is a question frequently heard about the band during the late 1990s and into the 2000s.

Conclusion

The rear cover is striking because of the Nazi-esque concrete hawk statue. It calls to mind the imposing statuary of the Third Reich. It certainly doesn't fit either the band's music or outlook but it does reflect the essential confusion within the band. The title comes from the American pulp magazines *Astounding Science Fiction* and *Amazing Stories* and the album is supposed to be listened to as if each song is a short story. Quite why there are so many instrumentals isn't explained. The inner sleeve is a fairer portrait of the band. It consists of a series of mock advertisements from the rear pages of 1960s-imported American comics. There are adverts for the Simon House school of music, Simon King's 'Pleasure Primer' book and it recommends Doctor Brock's 'atomic pile preparations'. These are far more in keeping with the bands humorous and parodic spirit than the conflicting covers.

Hawkwind influenced Krautrock and Hawkwind were, in their turn, influenced by that great German outpouring of music. Harmonia's 1975 delight *Deluxe*, for instance, is a clear forerunner to the keyboard and synthesizer sounds used on *Astounding Sounds, Amazing Music*. Brock was clearly a fan of the genre as he had recommended Can and other bands to anyone who would listen and even wrote the sleeve notes for the U.K. release of *Neu!* Of course, Hawkwind had also inherited Amon Duul II's bass player, Dave Anderson, in 1971.

Brock was becoming increasingly insular within the group and was only barely starting his new collaboration with Calvert. The rest of the band were enthused by Rudolph's dexterity and the wider musical palette that opened out before them. The album uses multiple writers and seems, as a result, unfocused. Turner, while expressing delight at the newly creative band, offers little to the mix in either his writing or musical contributions. Calvert, by contrast, had gained great confidence from his two solo albums and the variety of songs and lyrical ideas he was able to express, cleverly and succinctly, widened for this album. The full flowering of his lyrical mastery would make itself felt in the next two years.

Astounding Sounds, Amazing Music is the first, really mellow, probably cannabis-infused, Hawkwind album. It is both exploratory and musically colourful, but it suffers, obviously, from an almost complete lack of direction. The appealing amphetamine mugginess and sonic soup of previous albums have been overturned, and a clarity and brightness take its place, along with jazz-funk interludes. On the plus side, its more relaxed moments actually make it the most 'hippie' album the band ever made. After the somewhat harsh view presented above it may come as a surprise that this album is actually well regarded. Direct, increasingly commercial, lacking the clinging wall of sound that dominated earlier albums this sounds fresh, exciting, melodic and nothing like Hawkwind.

After an abortive attempt to sack Brock in 1976, the band entered a final tumultuous stage of hirings and firings. In short order Turner, Powell and then Rudolph left or were ousted. Turner's tenure was curtailed for various reasons: firstly because singers and soloists alike continually complained that he would play over them, secondly because he enjoyed the psychedelic jazz direction the band was taking and thirdly because 'he can't play the saxophone properly'. The final reason seems to have been that he was the instigator of the sacking of Brock. It also didn't help that Turner had barely contributed to the songwriting for the past few years.

The band slotted new bass player Adrian Shaw into the sessions for their new album. He came from free festival/Hell's Angels favourites Magic Muscle who had disintegrated after support slots on the *Space Ritual* tour.

Quark, Strangeness and Charm (Charisma, June 1977)

Personnel:
Dave Brock: vocals, guitars, synthesizers
Robert Calvert: vocals, percussion, Morse
Simon King: drums, percussion
Simon House: violin, keyboards, anvil, vocals
Adrian Shaw: bass guitar, vocals, handclaps
Produced at Rockfield Studios, Monmouth by Hawkwind, January-February 1977.
Highest chart place: 30 (UK)
Running time (approximately): 36:54

'Spirit Of The Age' (Brock/Calvert)

Starting, I would like to think, with the sound of a cryogenic capsule being opened and the occupant being defrosted, the noise appears to coalesce into transmissions rescued from deep space which educate the clone while it is being force-grown for the benefit of the song's narrator. This is only one of the daring musical manoeuvres on display throughout the album, although it is the most radical. The crackling radio wave guitar riff that surfaces from the maelstrom heralds a mid-tempo song concerning the marvellously affecting, and amusing, tale of a man trying to make love with an android replica of his long-dead girlfriend. Calvert gets to drop Morse code over proceedings in a nod to previous unmusical audio oscillators but with an added resonance due to the subject matter. Ending with a rather more serious plea for tolerance, freedom and an end to battery farm-like lives it is clear that Calvert's lyrical sophistication and creative industry were going to be essential to the newly revitalised band and the stripped-down sound allowed the full breadth of his words and voice to be heard. Gone were the days of musical sludge and indecipherable lyrics, the sharper sound reflected the sharper force of the words.

'Damnation Alley' (Brock/Calvert/House)

This is the epic of the album and benefits greatly, as does the entire album, from House's keenly hypnotic violin work. Beginning in a storm and then dragging itself through more interstellar transmissions the sprightly synthesizer riff is complemented by quick bass runs up and down the strings and sets off on a post-holocaust tale of a daring road trip through an atomic bomb scarred American landscape in order to deliver a vaccine to a beleaguered town several hundred miles away. The song name-checks Dr Strangelove and draws heavily from the novel of the same name by Calvert favourite Roger Zelazny.

'Fable Of A Failed Race' (Brock/Calvert)

A slow keyboard and sustained guitar lope through the dying embers of a civilisation; this has a stirring melody, multi-echoed voices and is musically dynamic and soothing at one and the same time. Quirkily short, there is no time for boredom, just a marvel at the variety of songs on offer here.

'Quark, Strangeness and Charm' (Brock/Calvert)

A genuine classic, this is Calvert's wordplay and humour on sparkling form, allied to a bouncy new wave tune that suggests Squeeze were avid listeners of this album. The group throw themselves into the song straight away and let Calvert do the talking, almost from the off. A bewildering array of references (from Einstein, Galileo and Copernicus to subatomic particles and 'Les Liaison Dangereuses') are all wrapped up in a tale of scientists with no luck attracting the opposite sex. Completely spurious as the lyric is, it maintains a remarkable hold on the imagination for its sheer exuberant brio which is only enhanced by the music. This is the hit single that never was but should have been.

When the band resurrected the song in 1993, they slowed it down to a ballad pace and spruced it up with a smothering of keyboards to replace the, equally dynamic, original recording. Brock sings the song beautifully and the sudden rock guitar and rhythm injections, spurring the trio into action, are entirely organic and give the song a commercial sheen that belies its new wave origins. The version on *The Business Trip – Live* is loved and loathed in equal measure. Its drug-like slowness and bright sound, cause opinions to vary substantially.

'Hassan I Sabbah' (Calvert/Rudolph)

Calvert was, notably, a voracious reader on a wide variety of topics. By 1976 there were a plethora of underground magazines, one of which was the uninspiringly titled *Seed*. Subtitled 'the journal of organic living' (later 'the journal of natural living') it was a very early vegetarian/vegan/organic whole foods digest, begun in 1971, that covered a wide range of topics. Chiming in with the bands' own ideals the magazine was undoubtedly within the group's orbit. In the May 1976 issue, there was a single-page comic strip by, now renowned, artist/author Bryan Talbot called 'The Influence of Hassan-i-Sabbah' detailing a lot of the background material later used in this song and illustrating how one underground source could be imaginatively extrapolated in another.

As to the song, House's astonishing violin playing reaches its wonderful Eastern apogee on this still frighteningly relevant song. It is a surprise House does not have a writer's credit for this tune considering he contributes stunning melodies and harmonics to this piece. Musically based firmly in the Middle East this is nothing short of a triumph and one of the songs that will stand the test of time for centuries to come. Calvert fuses together a thousand years of bloody history in a series of repetitive chants and a single verse:

Death unto all infidels in oil
Guide us o thou genie of the smoke
Lead us to a thousand and one nights
In the perfumed garden of delights

... before letting loose with a barrage of mystic imagery with a clear line being drawn between the Hashishin (11th Century fanatics, from whom we get the words assassin and hashish) and the contemporary terrorist organisations of Calvert's era (the Palestinian group Black September). Thrown into this mix is the long-running fight for oil and its derivatives (i.e. petrol and diesel) which still rages today (witness the Iraq Wars where the U.S. attempted to protect their vital oil interests), something that Calvert essentially predicted and for which Rudolph provides a highly memorable soundtrack. There is no hint of humour in the lyrics but a great deal of thought and power is evident.

'The Forge Of Vulcan' (House)

This is a cycling instrumental that prefigures the looping synthesizers and sequencer systems of the 1990s although the use of a genuine anvil as a rhythmic device gives the track an edge of authenticity that pervades the whole album. House again astounds with his melodic but inventive music, and he really does hit an anvil as a percussion instrument. Vulcan himself is the Roman God of fire and metalworking, son of Jupiter and Juno, who works as a blacksmith. Naturally, he has a forge.

'Days Of The Underground' (Brock/Calvert)

As its title suggests, this song deals with the early years of the band and the scene that spawned it. It features mentions of people from Hawkwind's past but doesn't descend into either regret or nostalgia, preferring to recount the tales as dispassionately as Calvert's vocals can achieve. As he sings in a jerky tone and the band add a metallic effect to his voice, it's no surprise that he succeeds in his intent. There are plenty of allusions to previous songs and the choppy rhythms echo the title track in an almost mirror-image fashion; where that is bright and almost pop-driven this is dour and fractured (reflecting the sometimes uncomfortable lyrics).

'The Iron Dream' (King)

The circling synthesizers and increasingly rapid pace of this brisk and brief instrumental are surprisingly long-lived as it reappears throughout Hawkwind's career, on live albums, and as segues or short interludes although its melody is slight and it is hardly memorable in comparison to the other pieces on this album. Nevertheless, it has achieved a longevity that is remarkable. In regards to the title, this is obviously from the metafictional alternative history novel of the same name by SF author Norman Spinrad, although the parallels between the two are very slight, to say the least, given that the book is a parallel worlds satire wherein Adolf Hitler is a dire pulp SF author in 1930s America.

Initially recorded by, and featuring a song by, Paul Rudolph, the bass parts on the album were actually overdubbed and completed by Adrian Shaw when Rudolph abruptly departed in the early stages of the album sessions. The full fruits of the Brock/Calvert songwriting team began in earnest here. Exceptional writing contributions from the remaining members of the band give this album a completeness and cohesion that would serve the band well.

In many ways, this is the true beginning of Calvert's dominance of the band. His lyrics, vocals, presence and theatricality all served the band extremely well, and it is his vision that steers the band at this point. The inner sleeve made the departures of Turner, Powell and Rudolph explicit and informed fans that 'we are back on course', although the subsequent disintegration of the band seems drenched in hubris.

Conclusion

Whilst musically active on the album Brock seems happy to take a back seat to the more creatively forceful Calvert. This results in a fantastically wordy, very much punk-meets-new wave musical stance, which sets this album apart from anything that had been heard previously. If you don't like the wall of sound mugginess and thick production of earlier albums this will make a pleasant change.

The studio sessions were productive, and both demos and finished songs were recorded for future use. These were, remarkably, the de facto *PXR 5* sessions as well. There were far more songs than were used on *Quark,*

Strangeness And Charm. A period of sustained, and extremely successful, touring followed and the band gelled well.

Two months after the album, the second novel of the intended Hawklords trilogy was published. Credited solely to Michael Butterworth, as it should be, and featuring a reduced cast of characters (Lemmy, Stacia and Moorcock were the casualties here) *Queens Of Deliria* nevertheless expanded upon the mythology created in the first book by suggesting that the outcome of the battle between rock and pop music (exemplified here by Elton John) would lead to the death of the Universe or the creation of a human Utopia. By this time, Earth is mostly a fragile wasteland straining to survive through the use of Hawkwind's benign musical influence. Again, the members of the band had no input into the novel, but the apocalyptic visions of the preceding album certainly chimed with the milieu of the books. The novel ends with the closing of gateways to parallel universes but ensures that the architectural jumble of their base of operations is, ostensibly, back on Earth. The Death Generator, however, is still active at the centre of the Earth and humanity is threatened with extinction or redemption once again. Although the third book, already titled *Ledge Of Darkness*, was never written an outline of the concluding part of the story was prepared by Butterworth and, it seems, shown to Calvert.

Meanwhile, Brock was, apparently, becoming fed up with the internal dynamics in the band and wanted to create a smaller, more mobile, unit that could play free festivals without the expectations of the Hawkwind name, again bucking the hindsight received wisdom, that Brock wasn't a particular fan of playing free festivals. Calvert began to show signs of a manic relapse that could only lead to a further hospitalisation and he, too, seemed to want to expand his range. Picking up a local Devon band called Ark as backing musicians the two set out on a brief tour as the Sonic Assassins which mutated soon after into the refocused Hawklords. There is confusion as to the reason for this name change: some say that Brock and Calvert believed the name was unavailable for use and settled on the new name to accentuate the ancestry of the music, others argue that the pair wanted to differentiate their new, concise, songs from the past and the Hawklords were the outcome. Either way, this doesn't appear to have been a deliberate tactic by the two men, but the end result was inevitable. Whether they knew it or not, Simon's House and King were reduced to session men, and Adrian Shaw was moved out of the band altogether. The newcomers were Martin Griffin on drums, bass player Harvey Bainbridge (both ceded from Ark) and keyboard player Steve Swindells (former solo artist and member of the band Pilot) and the last vestiges of the original Hawkwind were temporarily swept away.

Hawklords – 25 Years On (Charisma, October 1978)

Personnel:

Dave Brock: vocals, guitars, synthesizers, keyboards, bass

Robert Calvert: vocals, percussion, wobble board, didgeridoo, jaws harp, guitar

Harvey Bainbridge: bass, vocals

Steve Swindells: keyboards, vocals
Martin Griffin: drums
Simon King: drums, percussion
Simon House: violin
Henry Lowther: trumpet
Les McClure: whisper vocal
Produced at Langley Farm, Devon by Robert Calvert and Dave Brock, June-August 1978.
Highest chart place: 48 (UK)
Running time (approximately): 34:21

'PSI Power' (Brock/Calvert)

The album is largely comprised of mid-paced rock songs with eccentric twists, and this is a prime example with its heavy effects, reliance on acoustic guitars, and intriguing lyrical exploration of a then-current topic, in this case, telepathy. Musically it has that jerky new wave pulse that almost defines the era, coupling it with a terrific lyric from Calvert was a masterstroke. The chorus suggests that the four symbols on Zener cards (to assist with detecting those who are telepathic) are:

> Circle, square, triangle, wave
> I get them crystal clear by the hour

Unfortunately, while this holds the song together rhythmically, the correct symbols are actually circle, square, wave, star and a plus sign. Calvert tells a story of a telepath who has to hide their prodigious abilities for fear of being locked up and used as an experimental subject.

Of course, when Ginger Baker got hold of the song in 1980 Hawkwind hit the accelerator, and the crooned Calvert chorus became a Brock belter, and it soared into the stratosphere on Lloyd Langton's guitar, the insistent drumming and the combined harmony vocals. Nevertheless, the studio version here has its admirers and with good reason: the central core of the song is sturdy, and the arrangement gives it a harmonic weight. The presence of a lone trumpet on the tail-end of the song gives the first hint that Hawklords are a somewhat different beast to previously although this is just the tip of the idiosyncratic musical palette about to be offered up.

'Free Fall' (Harvey Bainbridge/Calvert)

From an instrumental Ark band jam this flowing, bass-led, drift is alluring and relaxed in equal measure, even when it scurries off into a choppy middle section where Calvert intones his allegorical ode to skydiving (in essence a desire to escape the bounds of the world and enter a state of limitless possibility) while the keyboards and synthesizers create an array of wind effects to match the atmosphere of the title and the feelings of floating weightlessness and endless falling that the words conjure up. This is a highly under-rated song where everything gels and Calvert adds his inimitable wordplay to a beautiful piece of music.

'Automoton' (Brock/Calvert)

Although consistently misspelt on the album cover, and in other places, this is clearly meant to be *automaton* which means 'a moving mechanical device made in imitation of a human being' and is the first real reference to the concept of the album. Brock provides a barely musical synthesizer backing with what sounds like early sampling (but is actually Calvert making disturbing voice noises). This is bleak music for a bleak concept. It leads directly into:

'25 Years' (Brock)

Originally written for Brock's long-gestating, and ultimately aborted, debut solo concept record about astronomy and the stars (and originally entitled '25 Years Of Solar Research'). Brock apparently decided that the faux 'Metropolis' concept of this album was the more interesting road to follow. Other songs slated to appear on the 'astronomy' album would, therefore, land up here (in modified form) and on the forthcoming *PXR 5*. Again putting effects onto Calvert's stuttering vocals, this punk/new wave hybrid rattles along on a slicing riff, a mechanically precise drum beat and a mass of whispered voices detailing the soul-destroying years of working in a factory that the protagonist has had to endure. While attempting to escape this life-draining drudgery the principal is given the sack and is then left to stare at the sky, quietly losing all hope but attempting to console themselves with the thought that they are rebellious and have no need to change.

'Flying Doctor' (Brock/Calvert)

This is the most left-field song on the album, and some might argue of Hawkwind's career, with its barmy instrumentation and bonkers lyrics. Ostensibly telling the tale of an Australian flying doctor (purveyor of medical services to remote areas) who spends rather too much time sampling the contents of his own medicine cabinet and rather less time treating an outbreak in the outback this has all the hallmarks of a one-hit novelty song except for the subject matter. Calvert sings in an Australian accent and throws in a selection of ethnic instruments (wobble board, jaw harp, didgeridoo) and then sells the humorously considered lyrics with as much sincerity as he can muster. Although Brock undoubtedly wrote the main riff, Calvert is clearly the brains behind this barking trip into his own comedy subconscious. The 2018 re-recording from *The Road To Utopia* ups the silliness quotient a notch but the original is already approaching unimpeachable. Needless to say, there is very little evidence of the album's concept here, unless it is that the 'hero' has such a terrible, mind-numbing, job that he needs to escape through drugs, and that seems a bit of a stretch. On the double album reissue, 'Digger Jam' appears to be a very early exploratory take on the idea, at least in Calvert's use of the vocal accent that turns up on 'Flying Doctor' proper. This bizarre interlude is cross-faded directly into:

'The Only Ones' (Brock/Calvert)

Back with the acoustic guitars, the harmony vocals and the dour pronouncements, this is a serious musing on bravery, heroism and hubris using the tale of Icarus as a metaphor for the search for intelligent extraterrestrial life which, the writer hopes, will come to save the world. Calvert imbues the tale with mythic force and the music bounds along, especially when the violin of House and the theremin-like keyboards of Steve Swindells carry the song to its fading conclusion. With its memorable chorus and hit tone, this is another commercial entry on a surprisingly pop-influenced album.

'(Only) **The Dead Dreams Of The Cold War Kid'** (Calvert)

This album boasts the only band track recorded without Brock (until 1997's *Distant Horizons*), an interesting indication of where Calvert might have taken the band on his own. The theme of espionage, in particular, the Cold War spy world of John Le Carre (rather than the intermittently silly and certainly fantastical Ian Fleming version), is brought to beguiling life in this acoustically-dominated tale of the two Berlins inside the two Germanys:

> In a town by the wall the machine gunners wait
> To type out the orders that seal his fate

Calvert sings as if he were in character wearing a trilby hat and trench coat and implies a furtive tale of skulduggery with lines like:

> Railway hotel with gun oil on the sheets
> The man at the harbour waiting in the streets

This isn't James Bond, but it is captivating, and Calvert's wordplay is insightful and poetic.

'The Age Of The Micro Man' (Brock/Calvert)

A sterling sequel, or at least in a similar musical vein, to 'Fable Of A Failed Race' this has the same pure vocals and keyboard-heavy musical setting of its forebear. Lyrically it seems to reference both the concept of this album and have allusions to the abandoned astronomy album of Brock's. It presents a stark and austere counterpoint to the humorous and playful words heard on that previous song. This prophetic futuristic society is grim and blighted by the technology that has enslaved its human population. Calvert strains on the verse vocals at times but the repeated '25 years of social research' line is the key to understanding this song as the conclusion of the album, taking its theme of societal experiments to the extreme and suggesting that humans are being exploited as cogs in a machine rather than being treated as individuals.

'Over The Top' (Bainbridge/Brock/Calvert/Martin Griffin/Paul Hayles)

This semi-improvised Sonic Assassins tune was captured live in December 1977 and is the first hint of the Hawklords concept. A weighty keyboard pulse heralds the improvisation but Calvert was under the impression that the next song of their set would be 'Master of the Universe' and introduces the song before having the rug pulled from under him when the expected riff never materialises. Rather than call a halt, Calvert starts to ad-lib phrases over the organically twisting music before he starts to sing/recite a poem which was either improvised on the spot or used elements of one he was working on at the time. The end result is a satirical anti-war polemic that is both affecting and inspired. The music is an adequate foil, but it is the words that raise this jam into the stratosphere.

Conclusion

The press release described the concept for the Hawklords album as: 'The story of Pan Transcendental Industries, a massive corporate organisation dedicated to the unividation of religious thought and modern technology. Pan Transcendental manufactures car doors, then removes the wings of angels and replaces them with the grey metal doors.' Joining the 'new' Hawklords was seasoned solo artist and team player Steve Swindells on keyboards and vocals. His short tenure with the band was profoundly influential but not in the way either he or the band, intended. He pushed them into an increasingly 'rock guitar' direction and gifted them with a perennial favourite live song. In the meantime, he slotted perfectly into the *25 Years On* sessions.

Taking its imagery from the film 'Metropolis', the album looks at the mechanisation of man. Although later brushed aside by Brock, with typical bluntness, as 'armchair Hawkwind' there is a lot to recommend this album (Harvey Bainbridge calls this their 'grown-up' album and suggested that *Live Seventy Nine* 'was back to being a teenager again') and the songs stand up to the very best of their output, which is why they are frequently revisited, even decades later. Calvert's muse is in full swing here, and it's a terrible shame that he had a relapse of his bi-polar disorder on the Autumn 1978 tour.

The sound is clean, clinical and clever and it has more in common with the predominant new wave musical tastes of the time than anything being produced by their contemporaries. The album cover model is actually Alistair Merry, the percussionist from Ark, who became a dancer for the Hawklords tour.

Swift and sure, this album takes just over thirty minutes to make its point and leave. It's the final great work by Calvert before illness again overtook him. In a remarkably prescient move, the band popped back into the studio days after the album was finished to remix '25 Years' for the, then exceptionally new, 12" single format. Although it never had any chart impact the fact that the band were continuing to explore new areas indicated their restless experimentalism.

Early in 1979, the band returned to the studio to record demos for the second Hawklords album. Lacking Calvert, who had both personal problems and another bout of illness, and with Steve Swindells departing partway through the recordings after being asked to front the band, the projected album never even got past the demo stage. Swindells wasn't taken with the direction of the new songs and almost immediately reactivated his solo career, with help from Hawkwind stalwart Simon King, old Hawkwind friend Huw Lloyd Langton and Van Der Graaf Generator's Nic Potter who all appear on his album Fresh Blood. Within months the Hawklords had ruptured; they had come to the end of their recording contract, and they had nothing to show for almost ten years of hard work. To their fans, though, it appeared much the same as usual: a new year and a new album; the hotchpotch of PXR 5.

PXR 5 (Charisma, May 1979)

Personnel:
Dave Brock: vocals, guitars, synthesizers, bass
Robert Calvert: vocals
Simon King: drums
Simon House: keyboards, synthesizer, violin, vocals
Adrian Shaw: bass, vocals
Produced at Rockfield Studios, Monmouth by Robert Calvert, Dave Brock, Simon House and Hawkwind, November 1977 (live), January 1978 (studio), June 1978 (Brock solo).
Highest chart place: 59 (UK)
Running time (approximately): 37:33

'Death Trap' (Brock/Calvert)

Fronting the album with the marked punk edge the band were apparently intent on pursuing, this song has a good deal of The Stranglers in its clipped music and scattergun vocals. Brock liberally spreads speeding rock and roll guitar solos over the charging music and Swindells even manages to imitate a screeching engine to compliment the lyrics. The words, according to erstwhile keyboard player Paul Hayles, were derived from Calvert's test drive of a car that he wanted to buy which ended in a crash. The opening line:

> In the back of my neck I can feel a strange sensation

refers to the broken neck suffered by one of the passengers in the crash. Calvert brings in biblical imagery of Christ going to his crucifixion at Calvary in an attempt to make the injury more mythic but devoting the entire third verse to cataloguing the vehicles many faults rather spoils the effect he is trying to produce. Hawkwind have attempted the song several times (1977, 1978, 1996, and 2012) with a variety of line-ups and have never produced a definitive version. The end phrase 'death wish' is always arresting in its finality and provokes a second look at the lyrics for its subtext.

'Jack Of Shadows' (Calvert/House/Adrian Shaw)

Slowing proceedings down with a scything guitar riff and a brief but unmistakable progressive rock keyboard solo, this owes another enormous debt to Roger Zelazny, this time his Shadowjack character from the book *Jack Of Shadows*. The 'sha-la-la' backing vocals and the jaunty tune belie the fantasy lyrics, based on the novels' tale of an executed supernatural thief out for revenge. This is a further attempt at a more commercial rock sound that, sadly, doesn't prove memorable enough on this occasion. Maybe it's Calvert's lacklustre vocals on the chorus, or maybe it's the music that lets it down, but this has the same lightweight feel as some of their earlier commercially-oriented songs.

'Uncle Sam's On Mars' (Brock/Calvert/House/King)

There is a tale to this epic spearing of American Imperialism: when Calvert first rejoined the band in 1976 he would recite his poem 'Vikings On Mars' over the motorik beat of 'Opa-Loka' (hence the writing credit for King) and, as Brock and House added their input, this evolved into the album highlight it became. Opting for an overdubbed live version rather than re-recording it altogether, gives the song its immediate feel, but some of the sounds are a little ragged. The swirling keyboard introduction is obviously designed to sound like a rocket taking off, and the fast-paced rhythm gives a surging sense of the eagerness of the crew to get to their destination and begin exploring. Playing President Nixon's historic radiotelephone call to the Sea of Tranquility and the astronauts on the moon is a glorious touch. The song title is derived from Gil Scott-Heron's 1970 poem 'Whitey on the Moon' and Calvert adopts a similar lyrical form even if the subject matter is different. Scott-Heron highlights the plight of the African-American poor in the United States and contrasts it with the billions of dollars spent on getting to the moon. In his turn, Calvert uses his platform to warn of catastrophic environmental collapse and the money that could, instead, be used to support the planet as it dies:

> Shoals of dead fish float on the lakes,
> But Uncle Sam's on Mars

Later on, just to hammer the point home, we get:

> Layers of smoke in the atmosphere have made the Earth
> Too hot to bear

The Earth might be a desert soon, America has left
The Moon
Uncle Sam's on Mars

Calvert also gets to satirise the inevitable Cultural Imperialism that would follow if Uncle Sam really did get to Mars by singing of McDonald's 'construction works', 'drum majorettes in white ankle socks' and hoping that 'you brought your credit card with you'. It all ends with the same swirling keyboard sound, but this time it suggests the howling emptiness of a dead world.

'Infinity' (Brock/Calvert)

With words originally printed in the *Space Ritual* tour programme, Brock tries an early shot at recording solo and the result is this slow-paced keyboard-saturated track which features strained vocals (Brock's music may be pitched too high for his own singing) and a lovely little acoustic guitar figure that gives this light piece a little more consequence.

'Life Form' (Brock)

This is basically an early indicator of future Hawkwind instrumental filler tracks. A psychedelic keyboard-dominated piece of whirling sound this, too, was recorded at home for Brock's fabled, but ultimately scrapped, astronomy album along with 'Infinity'. A saving grace is its brevity and the sudden cut of the music, but this is not a star in Brock's musical firmament.

'Robot' (Brock/Calvert)

This is a storming live song-with-overdubs which, with its thick sound, eight-minute runtime and repetitive percussive beat, recalls old Hawkwind but marries it to a stronger song structure and tones down the guitar in the mix, instead giving the space to House's affected violin squalls. The only real lack is the propelling drive of Lemmy's bass playing. Looking at a perennial Hawkwind subject, the spirit-breaking toil of the daily grind, Calvert postulates further by exploring the idea of 'nearly human' robots which could take over the world if not for the three laws of robotics laid down by Asimov:

> 'First Law: a robot may not injure a human being or, through inaction, allow a human being to come to harm.
> Second Law: a robot must obey orders given it by human beings except where such orders would conflict with the First Law.
> Third Law: a robot must protect its own existence as long as such protection does not conflict with the First or Second Laws.'

In Asimov's fiction, he finds ways around these, apparently sound, laws and Calvert hints at the same loopholes in his lyrics. Another profound influence on this song is Philip K. Dick; virtually his entire writing career was devoted to a single question: What makes us Human? The corollary of that is: how do we know that we are Human? This is the question that Calvert takes on here, slipping into the first person for the final stanza, after his previous, rather more removed, narrative voice. Repeating the individual letters 'R.O.B.O.T.' for the remainder of the track gives it the feeling of a mantra or a subconscious clue to the protagonists' real nature. Any fans of the film *Blade Runner* will see the parallels immediately.

The word 'robot' is from the Czech 'robota' meaning 'forced labour'. The term was first introduced in the 1920 play 'R.U.R. [Rossum's Universal Robots]' by Karel Capek, and it was almost immediately adopted by SF writers worldwide. While the play itself is obscure, Capek coined and popularised a term that is familiar to the whole world.

'High Rise' (Calvert/House)

J.G. Ballard (literary and SF author) wrote the 1975 novel this song is based on, although Calvert is known to have lived in a tower block in his home town of Margate. It is a cautionary 'Lord of the Flies' tale of a single tower block's descent into anarchy and barbarism. Calvert turns this into an invigorating social commentary about societal breakdown and the dichotomy that highly populated high rise buildings can create insular and paranoid people barricading themselves into their own apartments, like snails in shells. The lyrics concentrate on the more macabre aspects of the tale, identifying the building as a 'suicide machine' and explicitly singing about the murderous fallout from the disintegration of any kind of societal norm. Although House is solely credited with writing the music, Adrian Shaw contributes a sinuous bass part that actually lifts the song into greater realms.

'PXR 5' (Brock/Calvert)

Steaming in on a jittery bass drum riff this is almost an audio diary of the band's break-up in 1976 dressed up in allegory and SF tropes. Poorly produced (the rest of the drums sound like mattresses being slapped, and the vocals sound like guide tracks rather finished work) this is, nevertheless, a sterling little song with an explosive violin solo and a quirky pre-chorus. Quite how Powell, Rudolph and Turner felt about Calvert's lyrics:

> Three of our crew who were with us then
> Did not survive
> Their life supports could not take the strain
> And so they died

isn't known but suggesting they were dead was hardly a recipe for cordial relations.

'We Like To Be Frightened' (Calvert)

This was either a tribute to the kitsch Hammer horror films of the day or a nod in the direction of 1950s American drive-in movies. Given the lyrics name-checking Dr Frankenstein, Dracula, Dr Jekyll and Mr Hyde it's a close call as to which Calvert was referencing. This short, single-length, tune was already mixed for release but never saw the light of day, possibly because it was another new wave-influenced song that even came with handclaps and 'woo-hoo's' to accentuate its pop credentials. It fits into the 'Quark, Strangeness & Charm'/'Jack of Shadows'/'The Only Ones' vein of commercial pop-rock songs that were a feature of the band at this time. This was later re-recorded by Calvert for his solo album *Hype: the Songs of Tom Mahler* and it was just as much of a lame-duck there as it was for Hawkwind.

Conclusion

The original rear cover shows the inner wiring of a standard British plug. The coloured wire connections that are shown are incorrect: a small health warning sticker was added, but on the second pressing the actual wires were blacked out for safety reasons. Inevitably the original pressings now have some monetary value. You will be delighted to hear that the original, deadly, wiring has been returned to the definitive Atomhenge reissue.

Culled from live concerts, Brock leftovers from his astronomy solo project and the productive earlier sessions for *Quark, Strangeness and Charm* this album acts as something of a template for the future. The use of variable studio and live material on one album would become a regular feature from now on.

Fans were mystified at the time when they read on the back cover that 'THIS IS THE LAST BUT ONE'. The double meaning meant that most people understood there would be one more Hawkwind album and then it was all over. Actually, entirely the opposite was true: *PXR 5* was recorded before *25 Years On*, hence the statement.

4: Measles and Heavy Metal (1979-1982)

With the Charisma deal finished and the band in pieces, it was a major decision to organise a full-scale tour for November and December without any label support at all. Brock must have wondered what had happened: one moment he had a full band around him, the next he was looking at Bainbridge and picking up the phone. Instead of splitting the band altogether Brock seems to have been enthused by the idea of psychedelic heavy rock again, and the tour turned into a triumph.

The chief coup was the re-recruitment of Huw Lloyd Langton and Simon King back into the fold and the inspired casting of ex-Gong keyboard and synthesizer wizard Tim Blake. Blake brought his own light and laser show to proceedings, and the whole enterprise seemed destined to succeed. Taking tapes of the live shows to Bronze Records, the band were rewarded with a new recording contract and their biggest hit album in some time.

Live Seventy Nine (Bronze, July 1980)

Personnel:
Dave Brock: vocals, guitar, synthesizer
Huw Lloyd Langton: guitar, vocals
Simon King: drums
Harvey Bainbridge: bass, vocals
Tim Blake: keyboards, synthesizers, vocals
Produced at Rockfield Studios, Monmouth by Hawkwind and Ashley Howe, recorded on 8th December 1979 at St Albans.
Highest chart place: 15 (UK)
Running time (approximately): 45:10

'Shot Down In The Night' (Steve Swindells)

The sheer vital rush of this adrenalin-fuelled anthemic song blows away four years of increasingly anaemic studio albums that, for all their excellent songs, gave the impression that Hawkwind were taking their Grateful Dead comparisons a little more seriously than they should have done. Armed with this dynamic song-writing parting shot, the band never look back. Bainbridge proves himself to be a sturdy bass player, King provides his galloping rejoinder with all the vigour of a runner on steroids, Brock sings with renewed determination and plays marvellously, Lloyd Langton's scorching guitar breaks bring a commercial hard rock sensibility to proceedings, and Blake just about keeps up with everyone else. The crowd noise that greets the listener doesn't get in the way but adds a crucial atmosphere that Hawkwind are rarely able to capture on studio albums. Swindells gifted the band with a perennial favourite and, while the lyrics are a little convoluted (it appears to be about people under surveillance and the emerging CCTV society, although Swindells himself says that it is about rejecting the norm), it is the headlong thrust and the gorgeous chorus that makes this song complete. This is a terrific song to debut but not the last song to have its first outing on the album.

As for the song itself, it's a toss-up as to which is the better version: Swindells' is the better-recorded studio version, the more song-oriented and the clearer enunciated while Hawkwind's has the pile driver energy and searing passion only available on live albums. Ironically, it also contains some of the same players with both Lloyd Langton and King contributing to the live and studio versions.

'Motorway City' (Brock)

From here on in, the album just doesn't let up: the thumping 'Motorway City' has a sparkling guitar introduction and disguises a song about touring with SF trappings. Although taken at speed, this song really floats past, the band blazing away at the new song with fervour and just a little finesse.

'Spirit Of The Age' (Brock/Calvert)

This is undoubtedly the definitive live reading of this track although it has lost its scene-setting introduction and replaced it with a more avant-garde synthesizer-generated shuffling opening. Brock again handles the vocals well, even with the treatment applied to his voice, and the chorus suddenly gains an explosive band attack and an empathetic guitar solo that sounds as though it was always there. Goodness knows why but the lyrics have had a tiny tweak:

> [original version]:
> Even this doggerel that pours from my pen
> Has just been written by
> Oh, another twenty telepathic men

and now it becomes:

> Even this doggerel that pours from my pen
> Has just been written by
> Another twenty thousand telepathic men

'Brainstorm' (Turner)

Introduced by a descending figure down the guitar fretboard, this carries on the heavy rock reinvention of old songs that characterises the album. King, a veteran of this tune for several years, tears through this at a punishing pace utterly at odds with the previous live version. Throughout the album, Lloyd Langton's newly installed lead guitar lines embrace both melody and a sharp attack that raises the musical bar for Hawkwind, and its most interesting application is on this previously drone-ridden track which acquires a rather more song-like structure and sounds all the better for it. Instead of grinding along for ten minutes, it has patches of light and shade and a guitar line that shimmers above the crashing rhythm section, along with a subtle keyboard accompaniment that softens the song. Sometimes, updating a song can be a positive move, especially when you have players with the calibre of Lloyd Langton. By the time Ginger Baker was playing this revamped tune, he had incorporated an unrepresentative and uncalled for drum solo into the fabric of the song which many fans found irritating.

'Lighthouse' (Tim Blake)

To slow the album down, and showcase Blake's immersion in the band, this is an eerily atmospheric solo song that utilises his synthesizer skills to the full (and, in concert, the battery of lasers that he brought with him). It provides a perfect contrast to the heavier moments of the album but fits in lyrically as if it were written for the band (although it was actually originally recorded for the 1978 album *Blake's New Jerusalem*). The titular lighthouse is, according to Blake, a 'guiding star' for the human race, signalling out 'across galaxies' to bring us home:

> It's helping us and tuning in
> To realign our race

Prefacing the song with a verbal homage to *Star Trek* by way of a 'Captain's Log' entry is a lovely touch. Using a synthesizer pulse as an aural equivalent to the lighthouse itself is inspired. Blake's voice is an acquired taste in his later works, but here he sings with panache and passion and is able to carry the tune perfectly. The entry of the full band is almost imperceptible and yet it boosts the song in so many ways as it leads to the stirring finale. This is another definitive version of a song.

'Master Of The Universe' (Brock/Turner)

To follow that the band revitalise another old favourite and it again benefits from Lloyd Langton's incendiary and inspired guitar work, but this time the audience is given the opportunity to recognise the riff straight away. As with the other updates, this bursts forth like a sprinter and powers its way through in just over four minutes with only the musical breakdowns showing any sign of easing off the throttle. The uproarious clapping and surprisingly melodic round chant of 'Hawk-wind' ensure that the encore will only be moments away.

'Silver Machine (requiem)' (Brock/Calvert)

To tackle the rarely played 'Silver Machine' was another experiment for their newly installed guitarist. Given the band's oft-mentioned disdain for the song, it's not surprising that it appears in a version appended with 'requiem' which, after about a minute of the actual song, is cut short by the sound of an explosion that finishes the album. This is startling on the first listen, but it is a brave decision that ends the album on a high note, particularly with the increasingly inventive keyboards and lead guitar making such a short appearance. Various stories have been given for this truncated version: one has the recording tape running out before the end of the song, another has the band hating the song so much that they attempt to destroy it and a third suggests that the song made the album overrun the optimum running time of 45 minutes, so it was cut short. Whatever the true story, it provides a great ending to the album.

Conclusion

Always a wonderful live band, this album highlights the tremendous advance the band had made musically since their initial live album, and it betrays an exuberance and enthusiasm that ensures a new lease of life for them. A marvellous counterpoint to *Space Ritual*, this album is essential.

Levitation (Bronze, November 1980)

Personnel:
Dave Brock: vocals, guitar, synthesizer
Huw Lloyd Langton: guitar, vocals
Ginger Baker: drums, percussion
Harvey Bainbridge: bass, vocals
Tim Blake: keyboards, synthesizers
Produced at Roundhouse Studios, London by Ashley Howe, Dave Brock, Harvey Bainbridge and Huw Lloyd Langton, July-August 1980.
Highest chart place: 21 (UK)
Running time (approximately): 37:41

With the immediate success of *Live Seventy Nine,* the band went straight back into the studio for a follow-up. After demos had been made King's problems were all too evident. Personal issues, personality clashes and, above all, technical and musical problems proved his downfall. The first mix of the album was deemed unsuitable, and King was let go. In a panic, the band looked for a superb drummer who could perform the surgery on the album that was required. So entered Ginger Baker.

Baker recorded the entire drums for the album in two short (reputedly day-long) sessions, and the result is, according to Baker, one of his two favourite recordings ever. The album also powered into the twenty-first century by being the first album to be recorded digitally. 'This is a headphones album' trumpeted the back cover.

Digital recording leaves nothing to the imagination and loses all the noise that comes through on analogue. In Hawkwind's case, the new digital recording technology meant that everyone's playing had to be spot-on and the looseness of the past was temporarily lost. In return, the band stepped up to the plate, and the best-produced album of the band's history was provided to the label. The tones are crisp, the sounds are clean and the songs shimmer and glisten unlike any other album before or since. It sounds wholly commercial simply because of the beautiful sound achieved.

'Levitation' (Brock)

The title track sets the scene with galloping polyrhythmic percussion from Baker, exciting lead guitar injections and speeding acoustic guitar breaks from Lloyd Langton, lovely keyboard interjections from Blake and scorching mythological imagery from Brock. The song is about miracles: walking on water is mentioned, but the song is mainly focused on the act of levitating and how wonderful the narrator believes it is. Amusingly, Brock sings:

> I offer you this chance to learn
> Take it now, there's no return

which is training that might attract the Trading Standards people if you then fail to float in mid-air. Clearly, after the Hawklords disintegration, Dave was setting his songwriting sights on fantasy, mythology and a return to the science fiction focus that had served them so well.

'Motorway City' (Brock)

This has a slightly slower pace than the live version but is equally memorable. Lloyd Langton's guitar stands out here and all over the album while Blake proves to be the greatest synthesised noise generator the band have ever had. His playing style and melodic embellishments complement the dirtier tone taken by Brock. When married together, the effect is sublime. Baker provides a deftness of touch and a degree of finesse to the rhythm that contrasts markedly with the more straight-ahead rock drumming of King on the previous live version. This simple European touring song ('where you exit on the right') is nattily dressed up in the desolate post-apocalyptic lyrical trappings of 'Damnation Alley' while talking allegorically about a mundane subject. Coupled with a diamond-sharp sound and the subtle but sturdy rhythm section this is another extraordinary song with undoubted longevity.

'Psychosis' (Bainbridge)

An introductory synthesizer piece to the next track, this sound effects, alarms and spoken-word piece rolls effortlessly into the next track but is probably the slightest bit of music here. It does lay the foundations for Bainbridge's future synthesizer work, albeit in a short form. The word itself means 'a severe mental disorder in which ... contact is lost with external reality'. This is an excellent summation of what Hawkwind are trying to do, musically, but a bit over-dramatic for the title of a brief interlude.

'World Of Tiers' (Bainbridge/Huw Lloyd Langton)

Here we begin to hear the soon-to-be-ubiquitous song structure that would come to dominate the rock world for some time to come: the song goes through movements of fast and slow, quiet and loud which eventually reached its apogee in the 1990s with the Pixies and Nirvana. Hawkwind are again at the forefront of musical thinking and innovation at this point. Again Baker astounds with his delicate, intricate but weighty drumming and the keyboards echo House's violin work in a surprising musical homage. Although this is an instrumental, it feels epic in its scope, and the lack of vocals goes unnoticed.

'Prelude' (Blake)

This fluttering, bubbling, synthesizer piece opens side two in chilled form, showcasing Blake's melodic mastery and assimilation into this disappointingly short-lived incarnation. This acts as a breather before crashing into

'Who's Gonna Win The War' (Brock)

The undeniably antiwar sentiment here is taken at a mid-tempo pace as Baker provides a military shuffle on the drums and again showcases his uniquely restrained and jazzy style while simultaneously sounding like a big hitter. The combination is electric. This is just one more in an album of highlights. On the same reissue is a demo recording of the song made by the Hawklords and the comparison is enlightening: the bass remains the same, as does the vocal melody, but the keyboards are intrusive rather than inspired, the drumming is unimaginative and lacks the sheer inventive verve of Baker while the lack of Lloyd Langton's shimmering guitar presence is most keenly felt.

'Space Chase' (Lloyd Langton)

Heralded by synthesised computer noises, this is another instrumental dressed up in loquacious drumming and superb solos from Blake and Lloyd Langton. Always a team player this is Lloyd Langton's turn to shine brightly and he embraces the opportunity superbly with memorable solos, a sparkling song and excellent musicianship. This brings the total of instrumentals up to three but at no point does this become dreary or uninvolving, on the contrary, this is the sound of musicians stretching out and accentuating the melody unconstrained by vocals.

'The Fifth Second Of Forever' (Brock/Lloyd Langton)

On the original rear cover, this is noted as being from the film. Don't try searching for it, it doesn't exist. In a rather charming piece of naiveté, the band hoped a film company would pick up the song and use it, having heard it on the album! Lloyd Langton provides a classical acoustic guitar introduction over a gently babbling stream which Brock then punctures with an electric rock tune which is then, itself, bookended by the reprise of the acoustic guitar piece. It sweeps along with grand chords and rock drumming while Brock sings with aplomb of airy concepts in cautious rhyme. According to Calvert the fifth second of forever is spent thinking

> Of the vermillion deserts of Mars,
> The jewelled forests of Venus

which is pulp SF imagery at its finest (and could, perhaps, be used to describe the effervescent sound conjured up by the music). This track has also gone by the name 'Circles' (although no-one really knows why except perhaps that the song itself is curiously circular in its dynamics).

'Dust Of Time' (Bainbridge/Brock/Lloyd Langton)

This is a fitting end to a watershed album. Distilling the preceding songs into a single soaring guitar-lead tour-de-force (complete with the astounding instrumental middle section that is, independent of the rest of the song, known as 'The Island') this seems to channel Moorcock in the lyrics with its depictions of frozen wastelands, under-population and

> Queues of sterile mothers
> Waiting for inspection

while the chorus is rather more celebratory, even with its pessimistic outlook.

'Nuclear Toy' (Brock)

A contemporary b-side, this lacks the sure touch of Baker's drumming and, instead, replaces it with an early drum machine that sloshes along looking for a secure tune to latch on to. It is a lesser song from the sessions although it still catches the imagination: curiously it appears to presage the coming 'industrial' sound that would surface only months later. Referring explicitly to the Three Mile Island nuclear meltdown of 1979 and possible British equivalents (Brock identifies Windscale as a possible site of future contamination: it was later renamed Sellafield for public relations reasons), illustrating an avowedly anti-nuclear stance, this is both heartfelt and disturbingly prescient: the catastrophic meltdown at Chernobyl was less than six years away and, while it occurred in 2011, the Fukushima disaster reminded the world that nuclear power is a source of great power but has planet-threatening consequences should they go wrong. Brock puts his voice through effects, to make it sound robotic, and then attempts to sell the emotive and terrifying lyrics through somewhat deadened vocals.

Conclusion

This is a glittering, glistening album of hard rock songs so well produced it catches people out after the sludge rock of early albums. It is a pinnacle of the band's career, and its momentum kept them going for the first half of the 1980s.

The subsequent tour claimed more band members in sackings and personality clashes. Baker departed (but not before stealing the concert backdrop and, allegedly, doing a brief tour of Italy as 'Ginger Baker's Hawkwind'!) impishly claiming in the music press that 'the world's worst bass player has sacked the world's best drummer'. Blake had other things on his mind and kept phoning his pregnant girlfriend, especially when she went into hospital. Not really understanding what was going on or the emotional situation that he was in, the band let Blake go. It emerged later that Blake's girlfriend had miscarried their child around this time. In their defence, Blake hadn't spelt out the situation to his bandmates and the insularity of the rock lifestyle meant that small irritations eventually blew up into huge problems. The group of the time now all express regret at the way this turned out. Blake would not record again until 1991 and would not play with Hawkwind again until 2000. The band replaced Baker with ex-Hawklords drummer Martin Griffin, and that left Brock and Bainbridge to handle keyboard and synthesizer duties in the studio.

Unfortunately, as ever, further disappointments struck the band: their supportive record label Bronze was hitting financial troubles, and the band was dropped. Heading back into Rockfield studios for the new recording the band signed quickly with the studio owners label, Active, which was funded by RCA. This would be the band's last major-label adventure.

Finally, the band contacted Moorcock for poetry and lyrical contributions, now that Calvert had restarted his solo career with both a novel, called Hype, and an accompanying album. In addition to the words Moorcock supplied, he also contributed vocals for one song. Upon its release Brock talked up the quality of sound on offer, remarking on the subsonic frequencies buried in the mix and the wealth of 'weird sound effects' the band had utilised.

Sonic Attack (RCA Active, October 1981)

Personnel:
Dave Brock: vocals, guitar, synthesizers, keyboards
Huw Lloyd Langton: guitar, vocals
Harvey Bainbridge: bass, vocals, synthesizers, keyboards
Martin Griffin: drums
Michael Moorcock: vocals
Produced at Rockfield Studios by Hawkwind and Ashley Howe, June-August 1981.
Highest chart place: 19 (UK)
Running time (approximately): 42:09

'Sonic Attack' (Bainbridge/Brock/Griffin/Lloyd Langton/Moorcock)

Re-recording a poetic highlight of a live album as the opening track on their new label debut could be seen as either courageous or foolhardy, and the majority verdict seems to be the latter. What possessed the band to do this is unclear, but it was by no means the only poor revisit of an old classic that was to blight the band during this period. Given the wealth of material recorded around these sessions, it is difficult to see an explanation. Lyrically this still packs a punch and the deadening weight of Margaret Thatcher's first premiership is clearly audible in the clanking, eerie and uncomfortable musical backing. This is a harshly suffocating new version which epitomises the sound of the new album: metallic, gritty, heavy and pessimistic.

'Rocky Paths' (Lloyd Langton/Marion Lloyd Langton)

Curiously, Lloyd Langton's material is always more convincing when played by Hawkwind. Written around 1971/72 for the short-lived Amon Din this is a punchy rock song with a fine tune, great guitar and a punishing drum sound that pervades not just this album but the two that were to follow. Buried in the words is an optimistic, undoubtedly Christian, message that people only need to open themselves to something greater, but the path may well be rocky.

'Psychosonia' (Bainbridge/Brock/Griffin/Lloyd Langton/ Moorcock)

The band just kept on jamming in the studio after 'Rocky Paths', and this was the result. The title is somewhat impenetrable, but that's in keeping with the initial nonsense of the words. While the music quickly distorts into noise before the final semi-spoken verse, Moorcock spells out, phonetically, the phrase:

> T.h.e.y. a.r.e. t.r.y.i.n.g. t.o. r.o.b. u.s.
> O.f. o.u.r. r.i.g.h.t. t.o. c.o.m.m.u.n.i.c.a.t.e.

complete with swirling voices, disturbing sonics and those precise, click-track beholden, drums. The title either means sonic/verbal madness or, perhaps, Moorcock had an unfortunate encounter with a person named Sonia who turned out to be a psycho.

'Virgin Of The World' (Bainbridge/Brock)

A short bridging piece that presages the next album, this is all curling synthesizers, ascending keyboard figures and bleak industrial soundscapes that plods along until the crying guitar of Lloyd Langton lifts the tone. The repeated chant of the four lines of lyrics sets an undeniable post-apocalyptic mood which belies the questionable utopian allusion of the title.

'Angels Of Death' (Brock)

Following that with a grinding riff-heavy metal song about angelic beings destroying humanity is a clear indication of where everyone's head was at in 1981: nuclear devastation was only months away. This is one of the songs that resulted in Hawkwind being lumped in with the emerging New Wave of British Heavy Metal scene (Saxon, Iron Maiden and even Motorhead were placed in the same category) but, even here, they are far more innovative and eccentric than the rather more conservative bands mentioned. The lyrics may reflect urban paranoia but the musical undertow is definitely a step away from rock and roll.

'Living On A Knife Edge' (Brock)

This is Brock musing on the 'Big Brother' culture already infiltrating daily life. He characterises the state/government as an Incubus metaphorically impregnating sleeping women and giving birth to demons as a result. The lilting guitar introduction settles into a faster-paced rock track that has a great Brock tune, an exploratory middle eight and a nice vocal coda that leaves the listener wanting more, rather than hanging on beyond its natural life. Brock obviously feels the same way as he has revisited both the words and music of this song in later years.

'Coded Languages' (Bainbridge/Moorcock)

Moorcock returns to a favourite subject (verbal communication) and provides his best recorded vocal performance on this song. Lyrically he is diamond-sharp in dissecting the obfuscation and misinformation that, particularly, politicians spout and the devastating consequences that can result. Allied to his idiosyncratic but powerful rock bellow, this is a stunning riposte to the tepid 'Sonic Attack' that opens the album. It also parks the band in severely inventive musical territory with its mock-computerized beginning before the triumphant main course of the song rocks out with a decidedly un-Bainbridge like verve.

'Disintegration' (Brock)

Brock uses vocal echo and backwards synthesizers, to paint another black future for mankind. Short as it is this has the feeling of defeat and despair that permeates the whole project.

'Streets Of Fear' (Brock)

This is an unconscious part of a suite of dystopian urban collapse songs that, arguably, are as relevant to the present day as they were at the time of recording. Brock flexes his lyric-writing muscle to good effect here, and musically he stomps along with an undoubted factory machine sound to the rhythm section. Only the lead guitar sounds free, and even that gets smothered at times by the crushing drums and industrial percussion. Amidst all this, there is no sign of hope or redemption. Brock portrays a nihilistic society in the very throes of dying.

'Lost Chances' (Brock/Moorcock)

Shimmering in on guitar shards and rock and roll momentum this is a galloping rock song that attempts to disguise some of Moorcock's more pedestrian (even hackneyed) words with a tight vocal melody, but it is bogged down by the lumpy drums and wayward tune and never really gels. This is not one of Brock's finest musical moments, and it is a disappointing end to a variable collection of songs.

'Trans-Dimensional Man' (Brock)

A somewhat jaunty b-side to the main action, this bristles with vocal effects and would have made a far better ending to the album. The guitars create an uplifting tune, the bass works hard and the old audio generators appear to have been dusted off and cranked into use. Additionally, Brock goes straight for science fiction lyrics although they certainly recycle some key phrases from 'Streets of Fear' which may be why it was banished to a b-side.

Conclusion

During initial recording sessions, Griffin caught German measles, so the band had to work on keyboard and drum machine dominated songs that Brock had been working on at home. Sonic Attack was thus delayed by a month while Griffin recuperated. This album is characterised by its subject matter, urban collapse and bleak paranoia, and its thick, soupy sound that recalls the albums of the early 1970s. The album grinds, marches and thumps the listener into submission. Aurally it's a serious statement of intent. Along with the other RCA albums, there is a blanket use of electronic effects, processed sounds and added synthesised noises which combine to give the albums the feel of being trapped inside a factory with machines crunching away all day. This is why they sometimes get lumped together as the 'industrial' trilogy. Here is the initial evidence for a heavy metal Hawkwind.

Church Of Hawkwind (RCA Active, May 1982)

Personnel:
Dave Brock: guitar, keyboards, bass, vocals
Harvey Bainbridge: bass, keyboards, synthesizers, vocals
Huw Lloyd Langton: guitar
Martin Griffin: drums
Marc Sperhauk: bass
Captain Al Bodi: percussion
Madam X (Kris Tait): crying voice
Produced at Rockfield Studios, Monmouth by Dave Brock as Dr Technical, June 1981-February 1982.
Highest chart place: 26 (UK)
Running time (approximately): 35:29

'Angel Voices' (Bainbridge/Brock)

Sounding like pre-takeoff techno-babble from the flight deck of an antiquated spacecraft (reminiscent of those featuring in the 1930s *Flash Gordon* serials), and featuring 'computer' noises that appear to originate from the 1950s, this prelude aggrandises the astronauts and refers to them as 'angels'.

'Nuclear Drive' (Brock)

This aptly named song lets the full band take to the skies and from then on the album flies off in all directions. This is a muscular rock song, that would sit comfortably on either the preceding or following albums. It concerns, unsurprisingly, the landing of a spaceship and the recruitment of an Earthling to travel the Universe. It ends with much the same sound effect as 'Silver Machine (Requiem)' which implies that the spaceship has exploded or crashed.

'Star Cannibal' (Brock)

Given that this track follows an exploding spacecraft it doesn't take a genius to work out that the Earthling protagonist has gone from a life of adventure to the aperitif menu. Brock attempts to rhyme 'flesh fondue' with 'main course stew' in a grotesque image that conjures up many disturbing and horrific thoughts. The vocal melody has a similarity with 'Uncle Sam's On Mars' although musically it follows the thudding drums and synthesised stabs of sound that characterise the rest of the RCA era. Only the bright guitar and keyboard sounds, and the storming end section, bring it out of the mire that surrounds it.

'The Phenomenon Of Luminosity' (Brock)

Keyboards and synthesizers blanket much of this album and, as it progresses, Lloyd Langton (and even Griffin) disappear from proceedings to be replaced by ever more diverse and experimental sounds that aren't from any recognisable instrument. Employing upfront keyboards, this provides musical backing to a sample of John Glenn's radio transmission as he became the first American to orbit the Earth. The title is a reconfiguration of the words he is heard speaking.

'Fall Of Earth City' (Bainbridge/Brock/Lloyd Langton)

This song is spoken, rather than sung, and it recounts a short story of evolution/revolution from the dome-lead lives of the populace to a more agrarian lifestyle, open to the skies. It echoes some of the narrative of *The Time Of The Hawklords* novel, specifically its use of the phrase Earth City. Again the backing is mildly musical but lacking in the hooks or tunes that would elevate this above the perfunctory.

'The Church' (Brock/Lloyd Langton)

Twinkling synthesizers and bizarre samples (the crowd chant from *Live Seventy Nine*, the muezzin wail of the Islamic call to prayer, a snatch of an earlier musical piece from the album) herald the putative semi-title track although it can't outstay its welcome as it lasts barely a minute, before tapering off into silence.

'The Joker At The Gate' (Bainbridge/Brock)

A low-mixed piano chord is heard before the entrance of the drum machine and synthesizer combination which dominates the rest of the track. Another largely spoken-word piece this also has various cries and shouts from Brock and Bainbridge for no readily apparent reason (although it is safe to say that they appear to be enjoying themselves). The whole piece predates Bainbridge's solo work and encapsulates his entire oeuvre in less than four minutes. The constantly descending keyboard riff at least bears a semblance of musicality, but this is sometimes turgid material dressed up for a major release.

'Some People Never Die' (Brock)

This is, essentially, the soundtracks of the assassinations of Lee Harvey Oswald and Senator Robert Kennedy spliced together and set to anxiously stuttering music, complete with added breathless vocal effects. It creates a tense and uncomfortable space for the sampled speech to really hit home. This track has also been called 'Assassination' (from an earlier Hawkwind demo and a Brock solo song), not surprisingly, which features a different but less effective backing than is notable here. Brock has occasionally voiced his desire to produce music for films and TV, and this feels like another example of his ability. For all its oddness, this is one of the most successful tracks on this album. Marc Sperhauk's appearance came from a cassette he had sent to Brock; his bass part was extracted from the tape and included here, although it is somewhat hard to tell as it sounds more like a synthesised bass than the real thing.

'Light Specific Data' (Brock)

There appears to be an acronym problem here. The original demo was called 'Water Music', and the splashing sample that is submerged during the bulk of this meandering and clunky piece exhibits its true origins. This piece still sounds like a demo, especially when the same explosive noise is used to halt proceedings when it carries on too long, even for the musician involved.

'Experiment With Destiny' (Bainbridge/Brock)

This song is a simple rearrangement and re-recording of *Sonic Attack's* 'Virgin Of The World' with additional sound effects, a frantic drum machine section and a distinct lack of any lyrics at all, which were the only saving grace of its predecessor, although the 'lyrics' are printed in the accompanying booklet.

'The Last Messiah' (Bainbridge/Brock)

A plaintive keyboard and synthesizer piece this has the first recorded appearance of Kris Tait (many years later she would become Kris Brock) as the sobbing woman. Subtly affecting, this has the feeling of a final track. It is a brief but remarkably moving work.

'Looking In The Future' (Brock)

There is a return to the full band here, which reuses the 'Assault & Battery' opening couplet by Longfellow. This song can't sustain its inventiveness for long but Lloyd Langton, thankfully, makes his mark again (after remaining silent for side two of the album), and the band return to something close to their space rock sound. The sudden backwards vocals and music add an intriguing touch to a peculiar album.

Conclusion

The original limited edition album (of 25,000 copies) came with a new booklet from the band which featured a colour cover and black and white full-page fantasy and science fiction illustrations as well as lyrics and credits for the album. It was well-received by collectors and, because of the success of the album, the second edition came without the booklet thus making the limited edition claim accurate.

This is the first really focussed electronics-dominated Hawkwind album. Although it features the full band on several songs, it's basically a Brock solo album with Bainbridge providing solid back-up. The overall tone of the album is provided by the all-pervading ambience of synthesised sounds which saturates everything. It has the bleak industrial atmosphere of the previous album but sets it in a far more space-age environment. Although held in high regard by some fans, its paranoid electronica is hard work for a casual listener.

Choose Your Masques (RCA Active, October 1982)

Personnel:
Dave Brock: vocals, guitar, keyboards, synthesizer
Harvey Bainbridge: vocals, bass, keyboards, synthesizer
Huw Lloyd Langton: vocals, guitar
Martin Griffin: drums
Nik Turner: saxophone, flute
Ian Holm: voice
Produced at Rockfield Studios, Monmouth by Hawkwind and Pat Moran, April-August 1982.
Highest chart place: 29 (UK)
Running time (approximately): 43:56

'Choose Your Masks' (Brock/Moorcock)

This is a bruising heavy rock song that charges straight in with the machine precise rhythm section and keyboards creating a crushing blanket under which can be heard Brock's muted guitar before Lloyd Langton appears. Brock sings the words with urgency and care. The lyrics are from the same Universe as Moorcock's Elric character where Chaos and Law are in a constant fight, thus maintaining the status quo required. Both this song and

'Arrival In Utopia' were originally credited to Linda Steele on the album due to ongoing disagreements between Moorcock and band manager Doug Smith regarding royalties. They were credited to his future wife in order to get around the problem.

'Dream Worker' (Bainbridge)

This is Bainbridge again getting to grips with electronica but stretching it out for minutes on end. Cheekily the group steal a line spoken by Ian Holm as Frodo Baggins from the BBC's 1981 Radio 4 adaptation of *The Lord Of The Rings* (I somehow doubt Holm was remunerated for the 'appropriation', although his name was, naughtily, placed on the front of the original vinyl sleeve):

> I have come, but I do not choose, now, to do what I came to do

Frodo then laughs and Bainbridge throws in a small piece of narration before the musical content arrives in the form of backwards bass overdubbed with random noises, splashes of guitar and whispered words. It goes on interminably, achieving very little along the way.

'Arrival In Utopia' (Brock/Moorcock)

Another fine heavy rock song from the writing duo, leavened with incisive guitar from Lloyd Langton and the martial sound of drums that still suggest they are produced by machine. Overlaid with lashings of quirky synthesizer noises, both sonic and sub-sonic, the music echoes the dichotomy of the words: the optimistic verses are entirely undercut by the pessimistic chorus where the protagonist has found utopia and then gets 'bored mindless' by it. Utopia comes from the Greek and means 'an imagined place or state of things in which everything is perfect'. The problem with perfection is that it is unreachable, unattainable and, as noted, imaginary. Or, as Douglas Adams succinctly put it, 'people are a problem'. Nothing disguises the fact that this is a wonderful tune with a memorable melody, although this is another Heavy Metal nail in Hawkwind's coffin for journalists who weren't listening to all that is on offer.

'Utopia' (Brock)

This is a gruelling coda to the previous song, consisting of un-musical electronic sounds for a time and then an echoed phrase appears that goes on and on ad infinitum:

> If you want to get into it
> You've got to get out of it

It certainly feels like it carries on forever.

'Silver Machine' (Brock/Calvert)

A limp and lumpy re-recording that is far better skipped and then forgotten. Brock sings as if he has a cold, Lloyd Langton sounds unconvinced, and the dreadful drum sound continues to approximate a machine being hit by a wet sock. So, passing swiftly over this, frankly execrable, newly re-shone abomination (recorded, we are lead to believe, as a 'treat' for fans) we move on to...

'Void City' (Bainbridge/Brock)

This is a variation on the *Church of Hawkwind* electronica experiments, although it does, amusingly, parody Jan & Dean's 'Surf City' song with its 'Void City, here we come' closing refrain. This piece samples the opening speech from *The Twilight Zone* TV programme to give it some semblance of purpose but the musical backing is more akin to Krautrock artists like Harmonia and Cluster: the bright keyboard melody and repetitive groove are then subjected to overdubs which drag the song out until it finally reaches its nadir with the surf rock pastiche. Here, too, is the only evidence that Turner has rejoined: there is a bit of squawking sax audible on the fade-out. It is possible this track was intended to be a pun about channel surfing, but the clunky drum machine, severely elongated run-time and lack of any real satirical edge leave this in the barrel-scraping pile.

'Solitary Mind Games' (H. Lloyd Langton/M. Lloyd Langton)

One of the only saving graces here is Lloyd Langton's gloriously glittering music for this song. Taken at a walking pace, Lloyd Langton drenches the harmonics with picked notes and makes his play for Dave Gilmour's crown. Hawkwind add a complementary backing of lush keyboards and tone down the drums in the mix to present a genuine diamond amongst the filler on offer. Marion Lloyd Langton injects some psychology into proceedings with the lyrics exploring states of mind and emotions in a poetic manner.

'Fahrenheit 451' (Brock/Calvert)

A descending guitar plunges the listener directly into a marvellously unexpected Calvert lyrical contribution which is backed by a rampaging rock tune from Brock's deep musical well. 451 Fahrenheit is the temperature at which paper spontaneously combusts although Calvert also wrote a poem called Centigrade 232 (which is the equivalent temperature on a different scale, although it tends to be referred to as Celsius now) to signify the burning of early drafts. Based on the Ray Bradbury novel (or film) of the same name, this leaves room for a grand guitar solo but, typically, misses out the controversial bible-burning verse of Calvert's poem in order to abbreviate the song to less than its natural length, unlike other tracks on this album.

'The Scan' (Bainbridge)
Here Bainbridge revisits 'Dream Worker' again, although this is mercifully brief in comparison, and says all it needs to in a quarter of the time.

'Waiting For Tomorrow' (H. Lloyd Langton/M. Lloyd Langton)
This is Lloyd Langton's rockier but restrained set closer, and it lives up to the expectations set by his previous outings. While he writes great tunes and his wife writes fine lyrics, it is often only Hawkwind that can lift his songs into the stratosphere. It's the subtle keyboard textures and the rhythmic bedrock of the group that highlight the depth of their compositions. He adds a spark to Hawkwind and they, in turn, bring the best out of him.

'Candle Burning' (H. Lloyd Langton/M. Lloyd Langton)
One of a brace of bonus tracks from the era, this is thematically outside the realms of even a non-standard Hawkwind song. It is, nevertheless, a thumping tune which is only betrayed by its obvious demo status, lacking the keyboard/synthesizer overdubs or any hint of rhythm guitar that characterises the rest of the album.

'5/4' (Bainbridge/Lloyd Langton)
Bainbridge begins proceedings with another stab at 'Dream Worker' territory but, once a human cry is heard, '5/4' turns into a riff-heavy guitar song, in a tricky time signature, that doesn't quite reach the expected heights but surpasses a great deal of the actual album material. Bainbridge tacks on the same reversed keyboard sounds as a coda and also works in a small bit of speech to justify his co-write status.

'Radio Telepathy' (Brock)
The mid-paced drum machine opening and basic rhythm guitar backing immediately single this out as a Brock demo that, surprisingly, wasn't used on his debut solo release a year later. Some of the lyrics reappear in several later songs, most notably 'Right To Decide' in 1992, but it feels like a complete song as it is and could have occupied the space taken up by 'Utopia' if it had only been given the full Hawkwind treatment.

'Lato' (Bainbridge/Brock)
This track has clearly been worked on a great deal as it mixes keyboard melodies and backwards synthesised sounds from much of the rest of the album into a distinct instrumental track. It doesn't have the hooks that reward repeated plays, however, and it has the feel of a *Church of Hawkwind* cast-off.

'Oscillations' (Brock)
Another Brock demo, this *was* released on his 1984 solo *Earthed To The*

Ground album. Appearing here in its Hawkwind guise it has a certain sequenced charm that gets inside a listeners' head.

'Recent Reports' (Brock)
This piece may be a demo, but the full band contribute to this mid-tempo rock song, complete with whirling keyboard sounds and sharp lead guitar breaks, that could have been worked up into a great album track if the group had applied themselves. The lyrics are a little 'early draft' in their political stance, but they would have been tightened up for a formal release. This song is another undiscovered little gem and a further indication that the album could have been astonishingly different to the one that appeared.

'Lato Percussive Electro (Earthed To The Ground)' (Brock)
Electro is the word here. If Gary Numan, Depeche Mode or Soft Cell put out their early 1980s demo recordings, they would undoubtedly sound something like this, although they would probably sound superior to this early Brock demo. Musically this carries on the 'Void City' template (complete with Turner's saxophone interjections), but lyrically it starts with musings on video recorders and TVs before it uses an early draft of Brock's solo 'Earthed To The Ground' words.

'Turner Point' (Brock/Griffin/Turner)
This track, by almost universal common consent, is the worst piece of so-called music ever officially released under the name Hawkwind and, given some of the appalling competition, that's saying something. It is the sound of Nik Turner farting into a saxophone. For four minutes. It has a stupidly repetitive electronic drum beat added by Martin Griffin and Dave Brock claims a writing credit which seems not only undeserved but also, frankly, lamentable. When the band were scrabbling about in 1987 for any leftovers they could scrape together for the album *Out & Intake* they alighted on this monstrosity. Moving swiftly on…

'Ghost Dance' (Bainbridge/Turner)
Arguably more of an Inner City Unit/Turner-inspired affair, this has a mantric chant set to a tribal drum rhythm and lyrics reflecting the subject matter. It is named after the Native American ritual dance believed to reunite Native Americans with their ancestors in the form of ghosts. This, in turn, led to the belief that performing the rite would cause the corrupt invaders to be swallowed up by the very land they stood upon, and the Old World of their ancestors would return. As a symbol, the shaman created white shirts with the sun, moon and stars emblazoned upon them which were believed to be magical: these shirts would act as bullet-proof armour in battle. Unfortunately, they were very much mistaken, and the Massacre at Wounded Knee was the

direct result. The song itself was performed from 1982-84 during the Turner dominated period but has only been released in live form.

Conclusion

Although he rejoined the band around May 1982, Turner had very little input into the album recordings, and his contributions were limited to a smattering of sax. The dour outlook of the previous two albums is still firmly in place, and this album does, indeed, sound like the concluding part of a trilogy, although the band weren't to know this while they were recording it.

With almost half of the album devoted to electronic effects, spoken word, drum machines and further musical experiments this is not an easy album to love. Rather than integrating these pieces into the body of the album they seem to overpower the thrust of the record. Nevertheless, it has stood up better than other recent albums and has provided the band with some fantastic material.

The Captain, Dave Brock, captured mid-flow at the Lowry, Salford 2018. (*Chris Walkden*)

Left: *Hawkwind.* The aberrant surrealist fantasy cover for the debut album. (*Liberty*)

Right: *X In Search Of Space.* Barney Bubbles gets creative with a fold-out cover and the Hawkwind Logbook insert. (*United Artists*)

Left: *Doremi Fasol Latido.* The iconic Hawkwind shield makes its first appearance. That's Barney Bubbles again. (*EMI*)

Right: The statuesque dancer Stacia was a considerable draw for the band.

Left: The incomparable Lemmy, rock icon in waiting, singing 'Silver Machine'.

Right: Nik Turner in full flute flow.

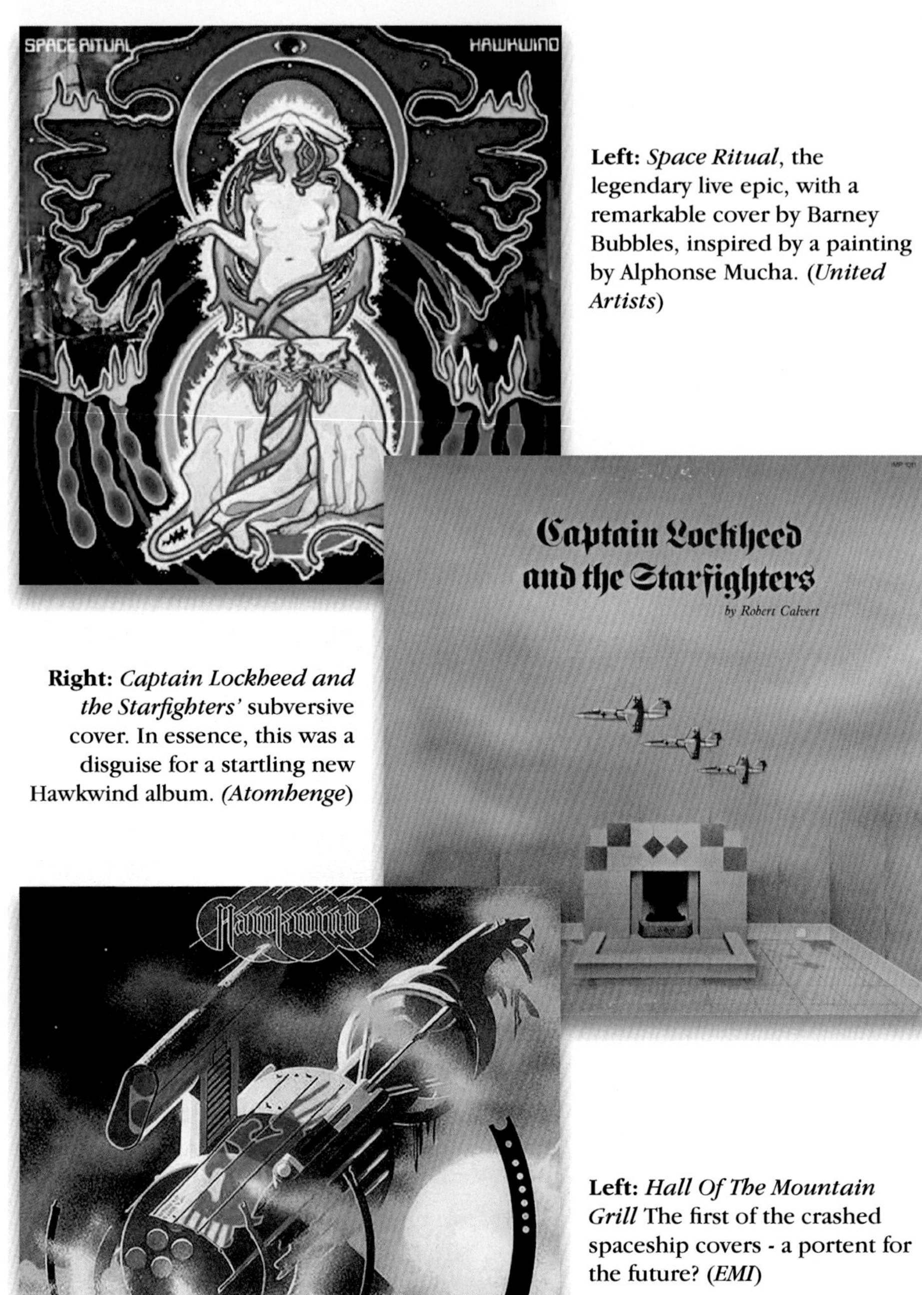

Left: *Space Ritual*, the legendary live epic, with a remarkable cover by Barney Bubbles, inspired by a painting by Alphonse Mucha. (*United Artists*)

Right: *Captain Lockheed and the Starfighters'* subversive cover. In essence, this was a disguise for a startling new Hawkwind album. *(Atomhenge)*

Left: *Hall Of The Mountain Grill* The first of the crashed spaceship covers - a portent for the future? (*EMI*)

Right: *Warrior On The Edge Of Time*. The album has a remarkable fantasy landscape that works so well even as a CD cover. *(Atomhenge)*

Left: *Astounding Sounds, Amazing Music* has a 1950's style painting, in which dope leaves are woven into the picture (and the album). *(Atomhenge)*

Right: *Quark, Strangeness and Charm.* This shows the inside of a real power station with all the confidential areas missed out. *(Atomhenge)*

Left: *25 Years On* The (perceived) homoerotic cover photo model is Alistair Merry, the percussionist from Devon band Ark. *(Atomhenge)*

Right: *PXR 5*. Whatever you do, don't wire your plugs this way. (*Atomhenge*)

Left: *Live Seventy Nine* garishly does what it says on the cover. (*Atomhenge*)

Right: *Levitation.* The cover recalls the spaceship designs of the *Flash Gordon* cinema serials of the 1930s, but without the budget. *(Atomhenge)*

Left: *Church Of Hawkwind.* A muted but symbolically rich cover for an album that initially came with a highly prized logbook. (*RCA*)

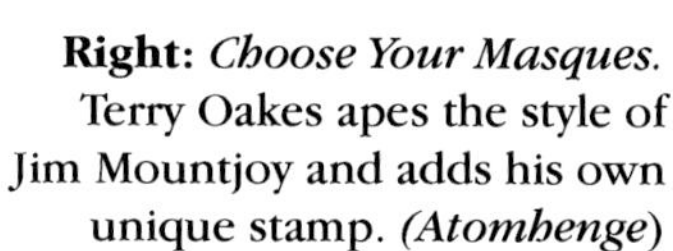

Right: *Choose Your Masques.* Terry Oakes apes the style of Jim Mountjoy and adds his own unique stamp. *(Atomhenge)*

Left: *Sonic Attack.* Famed artist Jim Mountjoy provided this striking cover. *(Atomhenge)*

Right: The promo for the 2014 'Sonic Attack' re-recording, featuring the stentorian tones of Brian Blessed, used fake TV news broadcasts.

Left: Another still from the 'Sonic Attack' promo, a little more handmade.

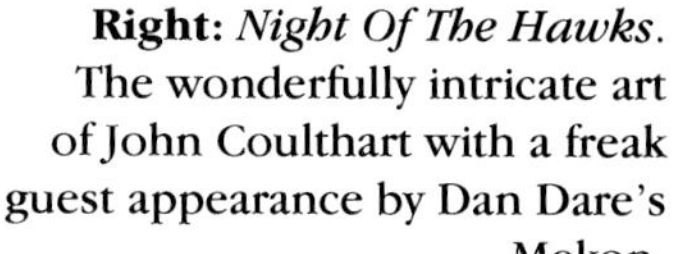

Right: *Night Of The Hawks*. The wonderfully intricate art of John Coulthart with a freak guest appearance by Dan Dare's Mekon.

Left: *The Chronicle Of The Black Sword*. A beautiful cover only appreciated in an LP-sized format. *(Atomhenge)*

Right: *Live Chronicles*. The cover enigmatically references the *PXR 5* wiring confusion, for some reason. *(Atomhenge)*

Left: The reactivated Hawklords, with sole original member Harvey Bainbridge, in Preston during 2016. (*Chris Walkden*)

Right: The Hawkwind-surrogate Hawklords in flight, with Ron Tree pondering his next move, in Preston during 2016. (*Chris Walkden*)

Left: Hawklords in Sheffield, 2019 featuring guest Nik Turner, newly promoted frontman Jerry Richards and Dead Fred replacing Harvey. (*Chris Walkden*)

Right: Niall Hone does the bass business for Hawkwind at the Albert Halls in Manchester, during November 2019. (*Chris Walkden*)

Left: Returning prodigal Tim Blake in 'mad-Theremin-Professor' mode on the 50th Anniversary tour at the same venue. (*Chris Walkden*)

Right: The thirty years (and counting) tenure of drummer Richard Chadwick is both remarkable and noteworthy. (*Chris Walkden*)

Left: *The Xenon Codex*. Wonderfully recalling the early 1970s with its original foldout cover and detailed artwork. *(Atomhenge)*

Right: *Space Bandits.* Another crashed spaceship, looking like the one from *Hall of the Mountain Grill,* with the current musicnauts illustrated. *(Atomhenge)*

Left: *Electric Tepee.* A great album deserves a great cover, and this looks epic on a 12 inch square of card. *(Essential)*

Right: *It Is The Business Of The Future To Be Dangerous*. An intricate Native American-inspired painting from Alan Arthurs. *(Atomhenge)*

Left: *Alien 4*. An impressive painted rendition of the surreptitious surveillance of the Earth by grey aliens. *(Atomhenge)*

Right: *Distant Horizons.* A bland attempt at producing a Hawkwind geoglyph based on the mysterious Nazca pictures that adorn Peru's landscape. *(Atomhenge)*

Left: *Take Me To Your Leader.* Influenced by the psychedelic covers of Ozric Tentacles, a bemused rabbit and peahen look on. (*Hawk*)

Right: *Blood Of The Earth.* The start of the computer-generated covers, with a distinct nod towards Norse mythology. (*Eastworld*)

Left: *Onward.* A reference to the Green Man myth - and similar to Roy Harper's 2000 *The Green Man* album cover. (*Eastworld*)

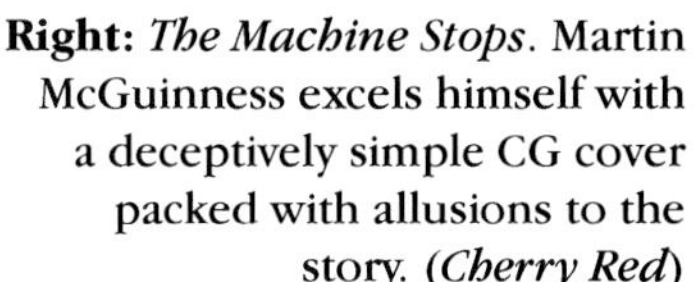

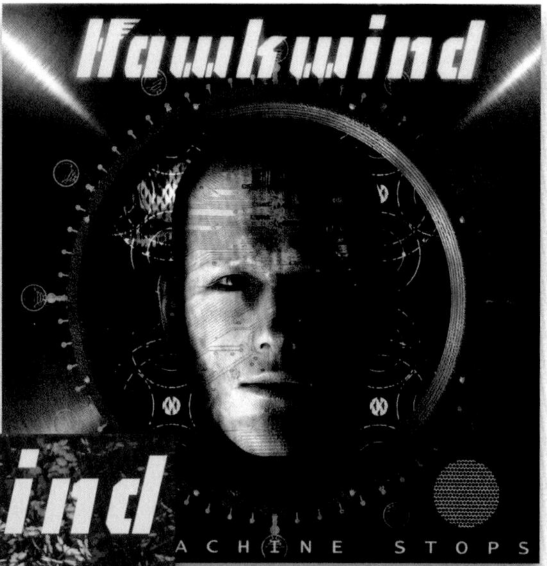

Right: *The Machine Stops*. Martin McGuinness excels himself with a deceptively simple CG cover packed with allusions to the story. (*Cherry Red*)

Left: *Into The Woods*. The darkly sinister conceptual continuation into fairytale and myth, again produced on a computer. (*Cherry Red*)

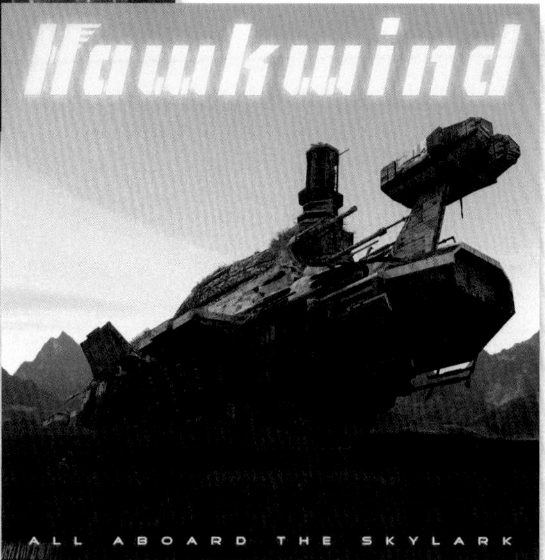

Right: *All Aboard The Skylark* Grass growing on the landed 'Skylark', in contrast to the crashed derelict version on the reverse. (*Cherry Red*)

Above: The eccentric Arthur Brown (looking akin to Ron Tree in our Hawklords picture) guesting at the Lowry, Salford in 2018. (*Chris Walkden*)

Below: Hawkwind with Arthur Brown. Mike Batt is crouching, somewhat incongruously in a Hawaiian shirt, next to the string section at Salford in 2018. (*Chris Walkden*)

5: Night of the Hawks (1983-1991)

While this period of the band remained fairly stable in its line-up there were still comings and goings: at Stonehenge Free Festival 1984 Alan Davey ousted, much to his chagrin, Bainbridge as bass player who was reassigned keyboard duties within the band. Griffin left after the completion of the tour following *Choose Your Masques* and, after a few fill-in drummers (including seasoned session drummer Clive Deamer, The Lloyd Langton Group's John Clark and New Model Army's Robert Heaton), the band settled on Danny Thompson Jr, son of legendary jazz/folk/rock double bass player, er, Danny Thompson (Pentangle, John Martyn).

The biggest comeback for the band was the return of Turner who, temporarily leaving his cartoon sci-fi punk band Inner City Unit behind, filled the frontman role that the band felt was required. Unfortunately, it was during Turner's most unbearable exhibitionist phase, and it quickly led to problems with both band members and fans. Few look back on his pantomime clown role-playing with much pleasure and his decision to have his clothes torn off nightly, leaving him naked much of the time, didn't endear him either to Lloyd Langton or much of the audience. He was unceremoniously sacked in 1984 and, on top of the loss of the RCA contract, the band entered the half-life world of independent record labels, endless compilations and stopgap live albums. The band's live appearances were well attended, but their songwriting muses appeared to have deserted them for a while.

Perhaps the reason for this sudden loss of confidence, credibility and musical muse was due to the shocking death of Dave Brock's wife, Sylvia, in January of 1983. Whether brought on by depression from marriage worries, money worries or family worries her suicide left a gaping hole in the lives of all who knew her. It is no surprise that Brock lost his songwriting libido. Aside from a mournful solo cover of 'Motherless Children' Brock never publicly referred to the event again, although privately he was a wreck for some months. It's probably not a coincidence that Hawkwind crawled to a stop around this time.

Months later the band reconvened. Directionless, they returned to their own mythology for inspiration, the first inkling of which was the *Earth Ritual* EP. Sadly, while the EP promised much, the intended absorption of Calvert back into the fold came to nothing, and the narrative thrust of the idea never got beyond a short treatment and some exploratory poetic drafts. Given the scant information available, there is still a real case to be made that the Earth Ritual was an early revision of the *Ledge of Darkness* book outline that had been around for some years. The suggestion that Calvert was being courted to return lends credence to the idea that he was to have a conceptual and lyrical role in bringing the project to fruition.

The EP itself did feature one startling return, Lemmy, in all his throat-ripping, bass-wielding glory, but missed out on a third returning prodigal. Barney Bubbles had been contacted by Turner for the sessions and seemed, at one point, to be interested in working with the band again. Having carved out a hugely influential career as a punk sleeve designer (largely for the ultra-cool Stiff Records label) he had amassed a fantastic reputation. In the midst of fruitful and friendly negotiations with his ex-partner for the bringing up of his child, Barney Bubbles committed suicide in November 1983, almost certainly because of a recurrence of his own bipolar disorder. Although not as well-known as that of Calvert it appears Barney too was subject to clinically worrying mood swings. This devastating second loss, within a year of the first, happened right in the middle of the *Earth Ritual* sessions. They, unsurprisingly, fell apart almost immediately afterwards. On top of the loss of Sylvia Brock, it's entirely understandable that Dave Brock's songwriting took a two-year sabbatical and that the band remained in the public eye only because of live compilations and previously recorded studio material.

The Earth Ritual Preview: Night of the Hawks (Flicknife, January 1984)

Personnel:
Dave Brock: guitar, vocals, keyboards, synthesizers
Harvey Bainbridge: bass, keyboards, synthesizers
Huw Lloyd Langton: guitar, vocals
Lemmy: bass, vocals
John Clark: drums
Robert Heaton: drums
Produced at Berry Studio by Dave Brock, October-December 1983.
Running Time (approximately): 15:58

'Night of the Hawks' (Brock)

Specifically written as an anthem, this is able to justify that aspiration with its startling guest appearance and superb hook-laden chorus. Lemmy lends a rock and roll weight to this self-mythologising and pumping rock song, which could have sounded cheesy but for his sturdy bass playing and growly harmony vocals. The celebratory chorus (complete with crowd cheers tacked on) and verses full of subterfuge and cataclysm definitely recall the atmosphere (and, indeed, the mythos) of the Hawklords novels rather than the putative return-to-Earth scenario suggested by the Earth Ritual:

> Between the radio stations
> A coded message heard
> No one knew the meaning
> All our efforts seem to fail
> But if they catch you listening
> Then they'll lock you up in jail

This is the precursor to the revelation of the message itself:

Then amidst the noise of a thousand people's talk
There came the cry 'It's the Night of the Hawk!'

This is a cry of freedom and undoubtedly recalls the Hawklords novels where the group was portrayed as heroic musical saviours fighting against oppression.

The wind was raging and the stars were black
We all knew there was no turning back
The gates of Hell stared in our face
Nowhere to hide in this wasted space

These lines place the action well within the universe of the books and, given this background, I suspect that it wasn't entirely coincidental that Baron Brock and the Thunder Rider were rejoined by Count Motorhead, on this occasion, for a rousing defence of humankind by the collective musical force known as Hawkwind. This has all the hallmarks of an early *Ledge of Darkness* try-out which was postponed when Calvert declined to take part.

Musically Brock sounds like he is enjoying himself immensely and the whole band play up a storm without taking themselves too seriously. Lloyd Langton acquits himself well, and the throbbing pulse carries the tune with aplomb. The original 12' vinyl issue is the version to own as, whenever it has been reissued on CD, the extended undulating feedback wave that finishes the song has been cruelly edited. Nevertheless, this is a jewel in the Hawkwind crown, even with the pedestrian production on offer.

'Green Finned Demon' (Brock/Calvert)

Opting for a slow-paced funeral dirge this Calvert poem is set to atmospheric music by Brock but doesn't result in another classic from the duo. Throwing in keyboard sonar noises and utilising Robert Heaton as a surrogate drum machine hardly inspires confidence and musically this has a plodding groove that brings the whole EP down. Lyrically it name-checks Captain Nemo, the anti-heroic star of Jules Verne's *Twenty Thousand Leagues Under The Sea*, but it never really grasps the lyrical nettle it requires. Recalling *The Creature From The Black Lagoon* rather than anything more profound, this unsuccessfully bids for affecting and instead ends up at affected.

'Dream Dancers' (Brock)

All this calls to mind is the sound of an asthmatic wheezer being mugged by a synthesizer-wielding Brock.

'Dragons And Fables' (H. Lloyd Langton/M. Lloyd Langton)

Ideally, the previous track should cut directly into this mid-tempo song that has a tricky lead guitar riff and a lovely refrain in its short length. Whether by accident or design the allegorical fantasy lyrics blend seamlessly with the next album project, although this was never the intention.

Conclusion

There is no sign of Turner anywhere on these recordings, and his absence must have been noted, even subliminally, as he was sacked before the next album.

During the Earth Ritual tour the band introduced several new songs, none of which were penned by Brock, including Lloyd Langton's 'Mark Of Cain' and 'Got Your Number', Moorcock's 'Damned By The Curse Of Man' and a revitalised version of Calvert's hoary 'The Right Stuff'. None of them seemed to fit with the Earth Ritual theme. The two Hawkwind albums released in this lengthy hiatus were made up of archive material, jams or songs from other writers. Zones has been described, fairly, as a 'rats arse' of an album and This Is Hawkwind: Do Not Panic is basically a chopped up 1980 live album with a 1984 Stonehenge live EP tacked on.

Robert Heaton was the drummer for New Model Army at this time, as well as being Hawkwind's drum roadie, and guested with Hawkwind at Stonehenge and live gigs as well as on this studio recording. Years later he died, following the recurrence of a brain tumour, in 2004.

By the beginning of 1985, Brock was returning to active duty and had instigated a line-up reshuffle and the second, and final, dismissal of Turner. Knocking the plans for the so-called *Earth Ritual* on the head, a decision was made to conceptualise an album from Moorcock's voluminous Elric novels. Turner had been part of the preliminary rehearsal and writing period for the project, but all that was scrapped and a new storyline was established.

The Chronicle of the Black Sword (Flicknife, November 1985)

Personnel:
Dave Brock: vocals, guitar, keyboards, synthesizer
Harvey Bainbridge: keyboards, synthesizer, voice
Huw Lloyd Langton: guitar, vocals
Alan Davey: bass, vocals
Danny Thompson Jr.: drums
Dave Charles: percussion
Produced at Rockfield Studios, Monmouth by Dave Brock, Harvey Bainbridge and Dave Charles, August/September 1985.
Highest chart place: 65 (UK)
Running Time (approximately): 37:12

'Song Of The Swords' (Brock)

Beginning with a conceptual hard rock song is a bold statement of intent that pays dividends only if the rest of the album backs it up. From the squelchy bass synth opening notes to the crisp drums and committed rock vocal from Brock the signs are ripe for a bruising entrance to a stirring album. Davey makes an immediate impact with his muscular bass playing and the song zips along with gusto, especially with Lloyd Langton scattering memorable lead guitar fills at every turn. Brock gives it a sterling chorus and begins the album, effectively, in the middle of a battle. Mirrored by the breathless rush of the song the lyrics appear to be from the viewpoint of the swords themselves (Moorcock created two sentient rune swords in the Elric books, Stormbringer and Mournblade) as they question if this clashing of swords is actually their version of paradise. Brock introduces Moorcock's world-view of an unending struggle between Chaos and Law and then overlays it with Moorcock's vision that the protagonists of this epic saga are ruled by their destinies:

> Your path is chosen
> You have no choice

Taking Elric and Stormbringer as the cornerstones, the album is a striking exploration of those philosophical ideas.

'Shade Gate' (Bainbridge)

This instrumental, rather than the experimental electronica of recent albums, is essentially a song without words and sounds all the better for it. Bainbridge conjures an atmosphere of tranquillity with a fluttering synthesizer line and a gentle keyboard solo that ends with what sounds like a metal-stringed harp being rapidly scraped. In the storyline, this is where Elric follows his evil cousin Yyrkoon through a portal to seek out the twin black blades of Stormbringer and Mournblade.

'The Sea King' (H. Lloyd Langton/M. Lloyd Langton)

With uncharacteristically heavy hard rock riffing from Lloyd Langton and a huskier than usual vocal, this song narrates the tale of Yyrkoon having his prisoner Elric thrown overboard from a ship and his eventual rescue by the Sea King due to an ancient pact. Elric is coming to terms with his imminent death but is forced, as if by fate, to call upon his saviour to return him to the surface. The pinging sonar keyboard sound makes a return, but this is probably the weakest tune on the album and appears to be a rock counterpoint for 'Green Finned Demon'.

'The Pulsing Cavern' (Bainbridge/Alan Davey)

This track, in particular, manages to convey the throbbing sexual subtext that, Moorcock admits, permeates the whole Elric saga. Bainbridge sets up a throbbing heartbeat background while Davey provides a sinuous bass accompaniment that suggests a womb-like environment, or something more sensual.

'Elric The Enchanter pts 1 and 2' (Brock/Davey)
A great mid-tempo rock song, this is literally two separate pieces welded together via a clever key change to create a single track. The words are adapted from Moorcock and based on a previous poem, 'Time Ship'. The lyrics concern Elric's reasons for embarking on a new quest; in order to test his magical powers and to stave off his increasing boredom and lethargy (for which he takes drugs to help him stay awake), he must have a new challenge.

'Needle Gun' (Brock/Roger Neville Neil)
Employing a basic Led Zeppelin style riff to accentuate the message, this anti-heroin stomp stands apart from the conceptual arc of the album although it obliquely references Elric in a wider sense as one of the multitudinous versions of Moorcock's Eternal Champion figure. The needle gun is the favoured weapon of Jerry Cornelius, the literary establishment's preferred version of the Eternal Champion. The song itself is another steaming piece of hard rock that benefits from the antiquated production of the '70s while the rest of the musical world was getting into gated drums, cheesy keyboards and over-using samplers. The words were ghost-written by American fan Roger Neville Neil, who would contribute further lyrics later in the decade. There has been a little speculation as to whether the lyrics also refer to the tattooist's art.

'Zarozinia' (Brock/Kris Tait)
Remarkably, this is, in essence, a soft rock ballad dominated by slowly pulsing keyboards and written by Brock's future wife. Tait tailors the words to the concept admirably and plays on the essentially tragic nature of Zarozinia and Elric's combined destinies with a haunting and lyrical interlude to the masculine action of the rest of the album.

'The Demise' ['Lords Of Chaos']* (Bainbridge/Brock)
This piece is a quick bridging synthesizer throb that has dramatic verbal narration from Brock (and Bainbridge as Arioch) to push the story forward, but it is hardly more than an interlude. Lloyd Langton noted afterwards that a few of these bridging sections were recorded and were then, at a late stage, given titles. This meant that they had become tracks in their own right and were therefore eligible for royalties. Given that two of Lloyd Langton's best songs were left unrecorded at this time, it is no surprise that the guitarist felt he had been sidelined and, perhaps, hoodwinked.

'Sleep Of A Thousand Tears' (Brock/Moorcock)
The sole credited Moorcock contribution; this has another fine rock and roll tune from Brock and a quirky set of words that describe how the hero and his lover sleep for a millennium, only to be woken into a world of confusion and tyranny:

Where the King of the world was a creature
Both man and woman and beast

which recalls nothing so much as Moorcock's Jerry Cornelius novel ***The Final Programme*** or, more likely, its progenitor, the W.B. Yeats poem 'The Second Coming'.

'Chaos Army' (Brock/Bainbridge/Lloyd Langton/Davey/Danny Thompson Jr.)

Another connecting piece that consists of drawkcab keyboards and an onslaught of hollow percussive instruments which possesses hardly any musical content but, in its favour, does sound chaotic.

'Horn Of Destiny' ['Horn Of Fate']* (Brock)

Another breathtaking riff from the fertile Brock fingers, this may be relatively easy to play but no-one else writes riffs so prolifically or as identifiably as Brock does. Listening to a barrage of pretenders there is not a single musician who can be as inventive as Brock within his limited range. His rhythm guitar hooks are memorable, and this is no exception. A slicing riff lifts a bruising and tragic lyric to greater heights and the extended end section carries the album off with a surging finality that ends in a shocking cry of pain.

'Arioch' (Davey)

While Davey has made no secret of his admiration for the incomparable Lemmy, another of his bass-playing heroes is undoubtedly Steve Harris. This charging instrumental is an Iron Maiden tune in all but name, dressed up for Hawkwind and given a concept-friendly title. It sounds like an undiscovered b-side from 1984's *Powerslave* album and would have fitted right in, Davey's nimble-fingered yet powerful bass providing both the melody and a dual lead in one dynamic package that charges like a bull elephant on the rampage.

*'The Demise' and 'Horn Of Destiny' were incorrectly titled on the original album release, according to Brock and others, so the correct titles are given in square brackets above.

Conclusion

This album was recorded in a great rush on a shoestring budget in a hair-tearing exercise that somehow exceeded all expectations. The band frequently slept on the floor of the studio and had little time for hindsight or overdubs. Although the production is drenched in the 1970s, clearly influenced by Heavy Metal bands of the time, it serves the adrenalin-fuelled heavy rock songs and throbbing instrumentals remarkably well. The album has the strongest set of songs in some years, and the writing credits are spread surprisingly even-

handedly. This is a masterpiece of hard rock order blossoming out of studio chaos that is only surpassed by its live album counterpart.

Live Chronicles (GWR Records, November 1986)

Personnel:
Dave Brock: vocals, guitar, keyboards, synthesizer
Harvey Bainbridge: keyboards, synthesizer, voice
Huw Lloyd Langton: guitar, vocals
Alan Davey: bass, vocals
Danny Thompson Jr.: drums
Mixed at Rockfield Studios, Monmouth by Hawkwind, recorded 3rd/4th December 1985.
Running Time (approximately): 76:10 (original) 91:28 (2CD reissue)

'The Chronicle Of The Black Sword' (Moorcock)

This is a straight dramatic recitation, by Moorcock, of his specially written poem which introduces Elric, the main character of the story. Accompanied by a flighty synthesised backing this sets the scene for the rampaging beast that is about to be unleashed.

'Song Of The Swords' (Brock)

Differing only from the studio recording in its beefed-up chorus guitar line, there is little to choose between each version. The story is set in motion as Elric battles against tyranny, with the Chaos Lords always at his shoulder trying to enlist him to their cause.

'Dragons And Fables' (H. Lloyd Langton/M. Lloyd Langton)

Fitting seamlessly into the narrative flow, this is Elric taking stock of his past and attempting to see a way through to freedom in his present.

'Narration 1' (Bainbridge)

This moves the story on, Bainbridge emoting that:

> Elric's cousin Yyrkoon has usurped his throne
> And has taken Elric, the weak one, prisoner

and then attempts to drown Elric by chucking him over the side of a ship. The sonar sound of 'Green Finned Demon' reappears here, and it carries on into the rescue song:

'Sea King' (H. Lloyd Langton/M. Lloyd Langton)

Toning down the heavy metal guitar riff slightly this pounds along nicely, telling

the story of Elric's acceptance of his approaching death and his subsequent extrication from the watery depths once he remembers a rune that can summon the Sea King to his aid.

'Dead God's Homecoming' (Moorcock)

Moorcock delivers a monologue in a dramatic tone that hails Elric's rescue and then maps out the next part of his quest: to battle with Yyrkoon and to restore his wife. Backed by swirling winds, the piece ends with a sympathetic guitar figure, apparently recalling happier married days.

'Angels Of Death' (Brock)

Speeding up the tempo and not locking the drums into a mechanical groove allows this song room to breathe. Lloyd Langton lathers on the lead guitar and carries the music to a surging climax that is over with far too quickly. It doesn't advance the plot to any degree, but it does reiterate the mystical backdrop and elemental forces at work throughout the story.

'Shade Gate' (Bainbridge)

Elric pursues Yyrkoon through this multiverse portal to search for the legendary twin black blades that could aid his fight with his cousin and, ultimately, bring him redemption.

'Rocky Paths' (H. Lloyd Langton/M. Lloyd Langton)

A questing song that suits its subject matter, even if the emphasis is less on finding the Christian God in yourself and more on Elric seeking the dread sword Stormbringer. Most lyrics are adaptable to changes in meaning and, given this story context, the perceived intent morphs into this fantasy world. Keyboards dominate this previously guitar-heavy song, but that is because Lloyd Langton concentrates on his singing.

'Narration 2 [Elric The Enchanter pt 1]' (Brock)

Brock describes Elric as he is caught in a trap that slows him down, leading him into:

'The Pulsing Cavern' (Bainbridge/Davey)

The heartbeat throb is loud and clear here. Elric is in a womb state and appears to be reborn at the end, leading him to feel like a God, his ego pumped up by his seeming divinity.

'Master Of The Universe' (Brock/Turner)

Elric proclaims his place as a deity, the multiverse his plaything, but all the while questioning the very reality of his situation. Musically this is played at a blistering speed, which suits the story format, and caters for the heavy metal audience the band were attracting at this time. It's no surprise that Hawkwind appeared at Reading Festival in 1986 and played several songs from this era, including this one, to placate the metal fans present. It didn't hurt that Lemmy guested on the Reading encore as well.

'Dragon Song' (Moorcock)
The ruling throne is referred to as the Dragon Throne, and this is a paean to the dragons that live in the mythical world of Elric. There are obvious echoes of the entire Elric saga in 'Game Of Thrones' and nowhere is that more apparent than here.

'Dreaming City' (Lloyd Langton)
The dreaming city is Imrryr, capital of Melnibone, Elric's ancestral seat. It is the home of the throne, and Elric's ultimate goal is to remove Yyrkoon and return to his birthright. The dreams are those of the inhabitants, the nobles, of the city and they are both monstrous and magnificent chimaeras that shape their pleasures. Lloyd Langton weaves the tale of the dying city and its decadent dwellers into a lugubriously paced and melancholic triumph, imbued with mournful melodies and a sense of tragedy. Elric's homecoming is unlikely to be greeted with any pleasure.

'Choose Your Masks' (Brock/Moorcock)
Cranking up the pace again, the armies prepare for war, choosing sides almost on a whim in this initial skirmish.

'Fight Sequence' (Bainbridge/Brock)
The undoubted weak point of the album this meandering sequencer and shouting piece really needs the visual of the on-stage sword fight for a listener to grasp the epic quality of the story. Now that this is part of a 2CD package this is a poor ending to the first disc, leaving the story somewhat in mid-air and a disappointing musical concoction in the ears.

'Assault & Battery' (Brock)
Blasting away the cobwebs of the previous track, Davey throws in a thundering version of the original bass part and then proceeds to re-energise the second half of the album. Lloyd Langton strafes the tune with guitar shards, and then he and Davey smoothly switch into:

'Sleep Of A Thousand Tears' (Brock/Moorcock)
Wherein Elric loses his precious love, Cymoril (Yyrkoon's sister and, presumably, also Elric's cousin), only to find himself in a new world a thousand years later (the Empire he is part of has a ten thousand year lifespan so this is a relatively short space of time by comparison).

'Zarozinia' (Brock/Tait)
Elric's new love, illustrated in the tour programme, is fleetingly glimpsed in this version of the story before she is kidnapped and ensorceled. This version stays true to the studio original although there are added crowd whistles and cheers to remind us that this is a live recording.

'Lords Of Chaos' (Bainbridge/Brock)
Elric requests help from Arioch, the King of Hell, as he fears being overwhelmed in the battle.

'The Dark Lords' (Bainbridge/Brock)
In order to thwart Elric's sorcerous powers, Zarozinia is turned into a giant slug, and then a ransom is offered: Elric must give up Stormbringer. This is a rattling rock tune punctuated by spoken-word declarations that ply straight into:

'Wizards Of Pan Tang' (Bainbridge/Brock/Lloyd Langton/Davey/Thompson)
Elric appeals to the sorcerers of the Isle of Pan Tang to magically restore Zarozinia to no avail. Musically this is a chanted section from 'You Shouldn't Do That' with the words changed to:

> She said, she said, she said
> She's dead, she's dead
> She said, she said
> She's dead

'Moonglum (Friend Without A Cause)' (H. Lloyd Langton/M. Lloyd Langton)
There's a beautiful guitar tone to the riff that permeates this ode to friendship and inevitable betrayal which makes up for the tragic subject matter. Moonglum dies by the sword of Elric and Stormbringer steals his soul. Lloyd Langton excels with a remarkable tune, and Marion Lloyd Langton moves the story on substantially with her lyrics. Shoehorning in a chorus that starts with:

> Moonglum and Elric hunting Theleb K'aarna
> Myshella now replacing Queen Yishana

and making it work, both musically and lyrically is astonishing. Whatever Lloyd Langton said about his personal preferences ('I like a good thriller!') there is no doubting his and Marion's commitment to this project. They elevate this concept almost single-handedly with their contributions. It is just a shame that there were no studio recordings of these songs. Again, this tune is segued directly into the next:

'Elric The Enchanter pt 2' (Davey)

Riven of its opening part, this still canters along successfully and puts Stormbringer back to centre stage which provides an impetus to the plot.

'Needle Gun' (Brock/Neville Neil)

The slight thorn in the side of this concept album, this explores more of the multiverse perspective of the Eternal Champion and, in passing, the drug-taking habits of Elric. Ensuring that the hard rock quotient remains high, this gutsy rendition makes its point and then departs.

'Conjuration Of Magnu' (Brock)

Brock declaims the opening verse to this song with an eclectic backing of bass rumbles and sound effects before storming into the tune proper:

'Magnu' (Brock)

The band drops the slow chug of the original and spring into charging life with this effervescent take on an old standard. Rather more perplexing is what the words have to do with the overall story arc, although they are suitably mystical, but the swift cut into the next song suggests that they are using it as a bridge to the rapidly approaching conclusion.

'Dust Of Time' (Brock/Bainbridge/Lloyd Langton)

An instrumental version of a sprightly rock tune this has extra lashings of guitar strewn all over it and a ruggedly organic feel in contrast to the digital studio original.

'The Final Fight' (Moorcock)

Moorcock revisits the stage for his concluding monologue and gives a sturdy performance which chronicles another battle, this time between the Lords of Hell, the dragons of Melnibone and Elric's own forces. Elric is sickened by conflict, unmanned by his losses and seeking the peace of Law that might give him rest. There is almost no musical backing, just a single ambient synthesizer sprinkle.

Moorcock, uniquely, takes time out to have a dig at the popular music of the time with a curious couplet:

> Meanwhile heavy metal songsters
> Cut themselves another line…

Whatever the reason, these lines stick out from the fantastical imagery surrounding it; it leaves the listener with some definite questions to be answered. Is this connected to the anti-heroin message of 'Needle Gun', only this time referring to cocaine?

'Horn Of Fate' (Brock)

And so, to the ultimate end. The story told, the battles won but time moves inexorably on. The sound of clashing swords, horses in panic and the lingering scream of Elric's demise bring this epic endeavour to a fitting conclusion.

The true zenith of the Black Sword concept, this album not only revisits old favourites in more energetic form but adds several new songs that are unavailable elsewhere, reinstates extra verses to a couple of songs and loses the ham-fisted 1970s production values of the studio version. The sound is clear, but the recording is not overproduced and it remains the only realistic challenger to the *Space Ritual* crown. The concerts themselves utilised backdrops, dancers, poetry readings, portentous narration and a full range of theatrical conceits to tell the entire story. On a minuscule budget, it was still a breathtaking spectacle for the full houses who attended.

The breadth and depth of the songs here are the epitome of the Brock and Lloyd Langton era of the band. *Live Chronicles* breathes, even if it is the sound of several men trying to give up smoking, and then sprints into life. This is a landmark album that proved the viability and longevity of the Brock-led band. And, of course, a sharp riposte to the carping criticisms from ex-band members. Flawed perfection from the band, as it should be. The one glaring omission from the setlist is the lack of Blue Oyster Cult's 1980 song 'Black Blade'. Moorcock was responsible for the lyrics, and it would have fitted perfectly into the concatenation of songs that comprise this album, even down to the hard rock groove and swirling synthesizer effects.

While Lloyd Langton was busy recording another Lloyd Langton Group album, *Like An Arrow…(Through The Heart)* the rest of the band reconvened at Rockfield Studios in January 1987 to put some finishing touches to their next album, *Out & Intake* and took the time to record a few extra tracks for this disappointing odds and sods collection.

'Cajun Jinx' (Bainbridge/Brock/Davey/Thompson Jr.)

While an interesting rock instrumental with a stirring build-up, there are definite holes in the sound where a lead instrument is required, Bainbridge doing his best to fill it with a lengthy keyboard solo. Lacking any hint of a Cajun flavour this is, at least, mildly rocky and undoubtedly melodic. There is a definite air of live-in-the-studio recording rather than the instrumental excesses that were to arrive in the 1990s although fading the tune out instead of giving it a definite ending is a sure sign that this was a rough version rather than a finished song.

'Flight To Maputo' (Bainbridge/Brock/Davey/Thompson Jr.)

This percussive world music exploration utilises several completely non-musical objects such as balloons and fire extinguishers. The backing chant has a hint of 'Ghost Dance' about it, but it hardly makes up for the inherent silliness on display here. While not entirely un-musical, there is precious little to recommend this piece. Danny Thompson Jr. 'played' the bric-a-brac objects as well as 'mucking about hitting things', and on the accompanying tour he came out from behind the drums to play a balloon solo. Needless to say, Lloyd Langton usually popped it.

'Confrontation' (Bainbridge/Brock/Davey/Thompson Jr.)

Amidst an urgent piece of instrumental music, there is an audio documentary, partially recounting the story of the 'Battle Of The Beanfield' (a clash between hippies, crusties and free festival freaks trying to stage a concert at Stonehenge and the Police who had orders to shut down these unlicensed events) trying to get out. It features samples of speech from radio news, audio clips of the Wiltshire Police Constabulary and interviews with survivors of the battle, all placed over an idiosyncratic rock backing.

The Xenon Codex (GWR Records, April 1988)

Personnel:
Dave Brock: vocals, guitar, keyboards, synthesizer
Danny Thompson Jr.: drums, percussion, vocals
Harvey Bainbridge: keyboards, synthesizers, vocals
Huw Lloyd Langton: lead guitar
Alan Davey: bass, vocals
Produced at Loco Studios, Caerleon and Rockfield Studios, Monmouth by Guy Bidmead, February/March 1988.
Highest chart place: 79 (UK)
Running Time (approximately): 44:11

'The War I Survived' (Brock/Davey/Neville Neil)

The crashing inventiveness of this song augurs well after the three-year wait for a new album. Brock and Davey are getting into their stride as collaborators with a searing attack and a triumphant tune. The only let down is the dated 1980s production (the keyboards are too polished, the drums sound electronic, and there is a veneer of over-production hanging over the whole enterprise). Lloyd Langton is left to fend for himself between the smothering drums and keyboard sounds and the strange recurring ticking-clock motif. Inspired by Kurt Vonnegut's novel *Slaughterhouse-Five* (an autobiographical and meta-fictional book concerned with the firebombing of Dresden in 1945 dressed in the time travel and aliens garb of science fiction), Neville Neil fashions an anti-war polemic with the sharp eye of a military man and a striking knowledge of both the book and Calvert's working method. Throwing in a couple of memorable lines ('buildings belch bombs', 'a bullet-proof bible') and using Vonnegut's own repetitive phrase, 'and so it goes', as a throwaway reference, this is a fantastic beginning to live up to.

'Wastelands Of Sleep' (Brock/Tait)

The group enjoys a rare outing into the emotional here but the rather slack keyboard and drum machine backing work in opposition to this beautifully melancholy depiction of depression, sadness and the healing power of dreams from the pen of Tait. The core of the music is confounded by the bright production sheen that plasters this album.

'Neon Skyline' (Davey)

This, in fact, is a combination of two great songs into one superb suite of music. The drum sound is all splash and no force, but Davey's tune shines above it, and his vocals blend in well to the Hawkwind sound, his debut solo vocal proving to be enduring. Davey has mentioned this was an early contender for the *Ledge Of Darkness* project but had to be used here as the band were so short of material when the concept was shelved. Integrating this into the following instrumental piece was an idea bordering on genius.

'Lost Chronicles' (Bainbridge)

Essentially a rocked up piano ballad, this appears to be an excuse for a majestic Lloyd Langton solo to shake off the torpor of the production and remind people why Hawkwind were so special in the first place. If Lloyd Langton intended to give Dave Gilmour palpitations about the recent torpor of Pink Floyd's *A Momentary Lapse Of Reason,* then he was going the right way about it. Switching back to 'Neon Skyline' for the final verse and chorus was also an inspired thought. The title suggests that this was an instrumental piece left over from *The Chronicle of the Black Sword* era and, given its quality, that could certainly be the case.

'Tides' (Lloyd Langton)

Unfortunately, this is where the album tails off and goes into a slow downward slide with a disappointingly twee instrumental guitar piece. Complete with the sound of gulls and a floating electric guitar cry, it sounds half-formed and bland in its intimacy. In demo form, it was a cast-off from the productive *Choose Your Masques* sessions (under the title 'See', or perhaps 'Sea') which shows just how scarce new material was at the time of this recording.

'Heads' (Brock/Neville Neil)

Originally found on Brock's solo *Agents Of Chaos* album, this loping bass-led cracker improves the situation, with its spiralling keyboard line, soaring lead guitar fills and disturbing lyrics. This is the tale of a literally disembodied head lamenting its enslavement for the use of others, in a typically pulp SF tale of brains kept in jars. Brock makes the most of the words, relishing every vocal nuance and disturbing image with the glee of a mad scientist.

'Mutation Zone' (Bainbridge/Brock)

Problems occur in the final dash for the finishing line with this appalling 'Dream Worker' rewrite. It bangs and crashes about without purpose for a few minutes while a snarky voice attempts to engage the listener with a muddled tale of mutations caused by nuclear radiation, Brock then singing nonsensically about the same subject for no reason. The final sound of water being poured out of a metal can makes even less sense. The production is at its most cloying and unbalanced here, although…

'E.M.C.' (Bainbridge)

That's before this monstrosity (perhaps standing for 'electromagnetic current') comes along and proves to be even more electronically experimental. This is where the album sags because there is no clear direction for any of these electronic excursions and, indeed, no purpose except to fill up space. The initial radio tuning section is the only part worth keeping, and it lasts only a short time before it is submerged into a sturdy bass-heavy rock section which could have been the beginning of something special but instead rolls on while all sorts of noises and effects are overdubbed inappropriately on top. The rhythm riff is curiously addictive but needs to have a full song bolted to it, rather than this time-wasting rubbish.

'Sword Of The East' (Davey)

Thankfully Davey contributes one of his very best rock songs to temporarily halt the decline. It has the sound of another *The Chronicle of the Black Sword* leftover, and the lyrics are a touching homage to 'Hassan I Sabbah' and that's no bad thing. There is even space for a violin part during the bridge section (where the sound of whinnying horses is heard instead) and time for a, sadly uninspired, solo from Lloyd Langton before everything fades out into the sound of the desert wind.

'Good Evening' (Bainbridge/Brock/Davey/Thompson)

The radio tuning section reappears here (it was originally from *Agents Of Chaos*), and the group proceeds to finish with this unfunny comedy mess. Chucking in mad samples, a short but spectacular guitar solo (why didn't Lloyd Langton get a writing credit for this?), silly lyrics ('just because we're has-beens'), self-referential jokes and stupid noises is a one-joke idea that might manage to raise a smile on first listen but the humour quickly palls.

Conclusion

The original LP came in a fold-out sleeve echoing that of *X In Search Of Space*.

The band remembers that the album was again recorded in a great rush when they were told that they needed a new album in five weeks. Davey recalls that the band used whatever they had lying around and made up two or three pieces in the studio, you can probably guess which ones. The album title comes from previous Hawk-lore: it's mentioned in the sleeve notes of *Doremi Fasol Latido,* and both Barney Bubbles and Brian Eno claimed, at various times, to come from, the planet Xenon. It's also a heavy gaseous element used in lighting and high-speed photography. The recording engineer for this album, Tim Lewis, is now better known as a member or ex-member of Spiritualized, Coil, Queen Elizabeth and Julian Cope's band under the name of Thighpaulsandra.

This is the sound of a band looking for a direction. It is noteworthy that 1989 was the only year when there was no released material from the band at all. Around this time rumours began to circulate that Hawkwind had been asked to provide the soundtrack to stalwart BBC TV programme *Doctor Who*. For the rollicking Arthurian-space adventure 'Battlefield' the band were, supposedly, to provide a stirring and dramatic musical backdrop to the swords-and-laser-guns atmosphere. It would have been fascinating to hear what the band would have done with this project, but it was only a rumour and, like most rumours, was entirely false.

Before the recording of *The Xenon Codex,* the band contacted Calvert again to see if he would be interested in resurrecting the final part of the Hawklords novel trilogy as a concept album, *Ledge Of Darkness*, which had previously been discussed. Given the lead-in time, there was no way the band could have made a concept album ready, so they used whatever dregs of material that were lying around. Calvert was prevaricating during negotiations for the long-shelved project which is why the idea was nowhere near ready. Calvert's latest studio album was the 1986 electronica of *Test-Tube Conceived* and hc had said for some time that he was concerned at the increasingly moribund nature of his solo work: this lead to his more rock-oriented contributions to the UK Amon Duul incarnation featuring Dave Anderson, Ed and Joey Ozric, Guy Evans, John Wienzierl and others which resulted in the overtly Hawkwind-flavoured *Die Losung* album finally issued in 1989. Given the stunning success of *The Chronicle of the Black Sword* album and tour and the decidedly hit-and-miss follow-up, this reborn concept was a natural next step and would provide the group with an injection of lyrical power that the story would undoubtedly require. The gestating plans were unexpectedly and definitively derailed by the bombshell of Calvert's death from a heart attack on 14th August 1988 at the young age of 43. In a cruel irony, the band were mid-way through a festival performance when they were informed of Calvert's passing, some accounts having Nik Turner breaking the news to them as he was playing at the same festival. Hawkwind had little choice and continued to tour but also put into operation a plan to re-establish themselves in America. A tour of small venues, that lost the band money, was merely the start of a four-year plan to put the band back into reasonable sized venues which could pay for themselves. In addition, the band used the touring to introduce their new drummer, Richard Chadwick, who hailed from a host of free festival and punk bands.

Although a short crossover happened, Lloyd Langton left soon after the recruitment of Chadwick due to disagreements about money and musical direction, or lack of it, as Lloyd Langton perceived. In Lloyd Langton's place came another accomplished soloist, the returning Simon House. Around the middle of 1989, a further contributor was recruited, who came as a surprise to hardcore fans: a female vocalist and performance artist in the shape of Bridget Wishart.

Space Bandits (GWR Records, October 1990)

Personnel:
Bridget Wishart: vocals
Dave Brock: vocals, guitar, keyboards
Harvey Bainbridge: synthesizers, vocals
Alan Davey: bass, vocals, synthesizer
Richard Chadwick: drums, percussion
Simon House: violin
Produced at Rockfield Studios, Monmouth by Paul Cobbold and Hawkwind, April-June 1990.
Highest chart place: 70 (UK)
Running Time (approximately): 39:07

'Images' (Brock/Davey/Bridget Wishart)

Opening with this complex, sprawling and dynamic suite the band set out their stall immediately. A bold, progressive rock multi-part epic peppered by mournful violin and a classic Brock opening riff it shows the sterling musicality of a band once branded barbarians. As well as introducing Wishart successfully, it also captures the live sound of the band in the studio. Moving through different moods and concentrating on Wishart's throaty vocals and deep lyrics, the presence of House in a leading role makes Lloyd Langton's absence bearable and adds a sonically diverse palette that had been sorely missed.

'Black Elk Speaks' (Brock/Black Elk)

Putting this genuine Native American reading against some tribal drumming had been tried before by Hawkwind (1973's 'Etchanatay'), but the new line-up proved inspirational. While a stirring piece of music in the early stages, it becomes transcendent when Wishart's vocals enter the fray and take the whole piece up several notches, and Brock's intimate guitar soloing, just adds to the mood.

'Wings' (Davey)

This is Davey's relaxed fretless bass ode to the plight of seabirds and it has an irritating keyboard thump that drags it down like the oil that covers the avian masses. What it misses is a menacing tone that would have lifted the song to greater heights.

'Out Of The Shadows' (Brock/Doug Buckley/Davey)
Bizarrely using a drag racing sample as an opening this is another lurching attack at rock music, and it speeds along nicely. The song is particularly noteworthy due to its unexpected ending when the word 'bomb' is echoed and stretched and faded out. American fan Doug Buckley provided most of the lyrics from a previous song he had written. He had sent the song to Brock who liked the words so much he and Davey wrote new music to back them up. The lyrics are like a writing exercise ('Use the words 'Out of the...' to start each line and see what you can come up with.') although they hang together well and create all sorts of startling pictures and juxtapositions. Live, the song was always much longer, and the classy reissue has added a full length 'live studio version' to show the song in all its great depth and completeness.

'Realms' (Davey)
It is followed by this strangely addictive bass guitar rumble which sounds like it was all achieved on synthesizers but, in fact, is nothing but bass guitar and vocals warped into fictional film soundtrack music. Davey claimed afterwards that he couldn't remember how he made it, but on his later solo material, he appears to have rediscovered the art.

'Ship Of Dreams' (Brock)
Covering a favourite Brock topic: the mundanity of urban life and the restless need for people to dream and escape, this has a clockwork beat that makes the point but lacks the edge that Brock usually brings to these pieces, particularly when you discover that the Titanic was known as the 'ship of dreams', even with the sound of gurgling water tacked on the end. House puts in a lot of sawing violin to give the track some bite but it never really strays far from its metronomic shackles.

'T.V. Suicide' (Bainbridge)
Finally, we end on an underwhelming note: to the accompaniment of a plethora of television samples Bainbridge again tries to disguise the fact that he has recorded another tired re-tread of 'Dream Worker', and this from a man who ludicrously claimed he didn't own a television at the time (leading one to question where he got the samples from and why he was so against television in the first place). Enough already.

Apparently the album sessions went extremely well, apart from a crisis of confidence from Chadwick and Wishart on their first full studio performances, and again a new line-up provides a new lease of life. Three-quarters of the album is the very best the band can produce, although the other songs recorded at the same time would have suited the album better.

'Back In The Box' (Bainbridge/Brock/Richard Chadwick/Davey/Wishart)

A bright production sheen covers these songs. This piece is sharp and spiky and a further hint of what a properly female-fronted Hawkwind might have achieved, although its jerky chorus is ameliorated by the always exciting violin playing of House who excels on the stretched out mid-section. Brock enters the fray late and starts singing some lines from 'Words Of A Song' (from *Agents Of Chaos*) before Wishart returns to finish the song off.

'Treadmill' (Dave Brock)

Ironically recycling the lyrics from Brock's solo track 'In The Office' (another raid on Brock's productive Agents Of Chaos project); this sets the words to a far more engaging soundtrack. The catchiness of the tune belies its deep cut status; it rewards repeated listens with its wistful world-weariness, remarkable violin presence and similar beat structure to 'Ship Of Dreams', although it eclipses that song in every way as the organic but metronome-tight pace reflects the boring day to day grind of uncreative work while the memorable guitar riff and inspired violin parts, suggest the true route out of the daily monotony.

'The Damage Of Life' (Brock)

Starting life as a crude Brock demo, this is expanded with a bloated and poppy keyboard introduction that gives the riff-driven song a little too much gravitas, especially with House's melodic violin interjections and almost doubles the original length. It has a quirky rock charm and is the only official Hawkwind version.

Touring without Brock

One of the supporting tours for *Space Bandits* is widely regarded as the most bizarre of the band's entire career: it occurred without Brock. Prioritising studio work for *Palace Springs* and other projects, Brock was temporarily replaced for a 24-date European tour that caused consternation to unknowing fans who thought he had retired, or worse. At this time, there was no internet, no Facebook, no band websites and no easy way to get news. Bainbridge and Wishart moved on from the band later in 1991, and the remaining trio decided they could carry on as a three-piece with their now highly computerised and electronic set-up the key to providing their signature wall of noise in the live environment.

6: Oldie Rock, Or, How Iron Maiden saved Hawkwind (1992-1998)

As the GWR contract deserted them, the band quickly signed to oldies specialists Castle Music. With a large bankroll and a huge roster of artists, the label was an obvious choice. By the time Hawkwind joined them one of the backers of the label were Iron Maiden's management company, Sanctuary, and they would be in receipt of the best Hawkwind album of the decade.

Electric Tepee (Essential, May 1992)

Personnel:
Dave Brock: vocals, guitar, synthesizers, keyboards
Alan Davey: bass, vocals, synthesizers, keyboards
Richard Chadwick: drums, vocals
Produced at Earth Studios, Devon by Hawkwind and Paul Cobbold, January/February 1992.
Highest chart place: 53 (UK)
Running Time (approximately): 74:27

'L.S.D.' (Chadwick/Davey)

From the double entendre of 'Light Specific Data' to the blatant single entendre on display here, there is a definite acceptance of the drug culture and its creative uses. This piece is genuine psychedelic rock which sets the scene for the dizzying array of mood shifts that are to follow. To a loping drum pattern, Davey adds a busy bass and dark keyboard motifs, while Brock scythes on a telling guitar riff before the song gains momentum and stretches out for several minutes of instrumental interplay before a simple but memorable guitar riff heralds the closing stages, finalised by fierce drumming as if it was the end of a live version. The only downside to this is the flabby drum sound which plagues the band for the next few albums and lacks the punch and force that is often needed to show the weight of the songs.

'Blue Shift' (Davey)

This is one of Davey's best synthesizer washes, coming on like a cut-price Vangelis soundtrack piece. It oozes slowly through shifting atmospheres although it carries on for a little longer than necessary. Alluding to the 'redshift', whereby studying the patterns of light distortion into the red/infrared spectrum can allow scientists to calculate how fast distant objects (like stars) are moving, Davey suggests that we can also look at the blue/ultraviolet end of the spectrum.

'Death Of War' (Brock/Mark Rowntree)

Brock utters this spoken word tirade, backed by a slow-moving synthesised martial beat and the sound effects of hysterical laughter, explosions, jet aircraft and children chanting. The co-writing credit is for convicted US serial killer Mark Rowntree, imprisoned for life in June 1976, who had sent some of his poems to Brock and had this one set to music. The words are a serious look at an age-old subject but still have something to say.

'The Secret Agent' (Brock)

This album contains several moments where Hawkwind remember that they are a rock band and this is where it begins. This is an affectionate tribute to the character-led lyrical conceits and razor-sharp wordplay of Calvert. This first, and third person tale of a spy has all the hallmarks of a Brock/Calvert classic with the addition of a seriously committed rock backing. Lyrically, it is an elegant riposte to '(Only) The Dead Dreams of the Cold War Kid'. Referring directly to Sean Connery's early Bond appearances:

> I've got an old, worn Trilby hat
> That doesn't keep me dry

along with throwing in mentions of spy staples like cyanide pills, trench coats, dark shades and skin-of-the-teeth getaways:

> I'm always getting in tight spots
> I manage to escape
> By either jumping off a train
> Or swimming in a lake

Brock surpasses himself with his witty words and committed delivery. Explosive drums announce the juggernaut rhythm and riff which career throughout the song, barely easing off the throttle for the inventive middle eight before returning to the main theme and the surprise ending: it just stops, as if a piece of the recording tape has been cut off.

'Garden Pests' (Brock/Davey)

Adding variety to the album are short and long instrumentals, inspired by the vogue for ambient interludes, that contrasts nicely with the rockier elements. Greeted with the sound of an old telephone ringing, and then a synthesised sax squawk and chirruping insects this plunges into a fast tempo drum rhythm and an upfront two note organ dash.

'Space Dust' (Davey)

There is a strange 1970s children's confection called 'Space Dust' which felt like little crackling explosions on the tongue when it was eaten. Bowing to American cultural imperialism, the same substance is now known as 'popping candy' and has reappeared in chocolate bars and ice cream. Davey may be referencing this, or he might be thinking of actual dust in space. With a stirring swirl of synthesizer and keyboards, it suggests the latter option is more accurate (although the twinkling sounds could well be related to the sensations felt from the sweet). Davey then rounds off with a heavily treated spoken section that lacks any musical hook.

'Snake Dance' (Bainbridge/Brock/Chadwick/Davey)

Written and first recorded before Bainbridge departed, this instrumental lacks his maverick musical spark and the integral violin of House that appears on the original. That synthesised saxophone sound reappears, to complement the Eastern melody and plodding Arabic-dance pace, but is a pale replacement for the original violin part. By the time the stirring keyboards come in the end is almost nigh and the piece fades out on a babbling stream.

'Mask Of Morning' ['Mirror Of Illusion'] (Brock)

This is a retooled and radically updated version of 'Mirror Of Illusion' which steams along and sounds both commercial and quintessentially Hawkwind. The words concern the breakdown of an acid-ravaged mind. Given the date it was originally written it may well refer to Syd Barrett and his disappearance from Pink Floyd. Musically, this is a blistering and straight-ahead rock song with a long breakdown in the coda that captures the spirit of the lyrics. Utilising a barrage of synthesizer and keyboard sounds bubbling over the bruisingly tight rhythm section this deserves its rearrangement and re-recording as it utterly surpasses the original. Hawkwind, and Brock, may often be chided for producing new versions of old material but, occasionally, the reinvention is entirely justified, as it is here.

'Rites Of Netherworld' (Brock)

A very brief interval of pompous keyboards that, it has been suggested is an attempt to play Stravinsky's 'Rite Of Spring'.

'Don't Understand' (Brock/Chadwick/Davey)

This is a slower synthesizer and rhythmic rock song that features indecipherable spoken words low in the mix and waves of guitar and keyboards. Exploratory in nature, and titled because of the complexity of the MIDI manual that the trio were studying, this would be equally at home on the next album.

'Sadness Runs Deep' (Brock/Tait)

With another heartfelt lyric, Tait focuses bitterly on the break-up of a relationship and the negative feelings it brings. Musically dominated by cycling Eastern-influenced keyboards rather than guitars but with a pounding rock backing for the chorus, this bears more than a passing resemblance to 'Wastelands Of Sleep' which it consciously echoes in the words.

'Right To Decide' (Brock/Davey)

By far the most contentious piece on the album this is also an undoubted musical highlight. A furiously rocking sequencer, drums and bass song it once again affirmed the band's relevance to the decade. A memorable chorus combines with a roaring tune and results in a surprisingly commercial rock song. Adopting a political tone, Brock rails against the rules and restrictions that are placed on people and upbraids those who sit at home watching TV or playing on their computers for not participating in society. The version appearing on the album has lyrics adapted from Brock's *Agents Of Chaos* song 'Hi-Tech Cities' and cuts out the controversial third verse altogether, merely repeating the first verse again. The absent verse dealt with a real incident: Albert Dryden had been in contention with the County Durham planning authorities for some time about his illegally built house. The Council had condemned the property, but Dryden was determined to defend his property. In the full glare of the media, a TV crew captured the entire scene as it unfolded; this morality tale of a man guarding his home reached a tragic conclusion when Dryden murdered the local council official who had come to evict him. Somehow the lyrical details became known to the relatives of both the men involved and Brock blocked the verse in recognition of the family's objections. Nevertheless, even in this abbreviated form, the song itself stands as a timely reminder that Hawkwind were still a highly creative and musical force.

'Going To Hawaii' (Brock/Chadwick/Davey)

Inspired by Brock's delight at his Hawaiian holiday (believe me, he will return to this subject several times over the next few years) this instrumental seeks to invoke the tropical atmosphere of the island with ambient keyboards and a tribal rhythm, along with the wash of the sea upon the shore. Stretching the track through more than seven minutes is an attempt to aid the listener's relaxation and promote its use as chill-out music. Unfortunately, it is a bit too sequenced and it has just a little too much going on to qualify as New Age music.

'Electric Tepee' (Brock)

Finally, the title track uses unexpected noises, a simplistic two-note bass line, chanting and Native American-inspired drumming to round out the sound. It finishes proceedings with a dash of human warmth and spirituality that stands alongside the headlong technological rush of the rest of the songs.

Conclusion

In view of the mass of material available to the band, it was lucky that they could finally spend the time they required by recording at Brock's newly installed home studio. Freed from the constraints of writing for many and various people, the band rose to the challenge of working as a three-piece and explored all sorts of territory that they had previously avoided. It is another genre-busting landmark album, that brims with vitality and restless exploration.

Early in 1993, the band were contacted by publicist and promoter Jon Beast. He was organising a series of singles, each featuring unusual collaborations, in aid of homeless charities. Other bands who recorded versions of The Rolling Stones 'Gimme Shelter' were New Model Army with Tom Jones, Thunder and nine others. Hawkwind recorded their version with Page 3 pin-up and, later singer, Samantha Fox on vocals!

It Is The Business Of The Future To Be Dangerous (Essential, October 1993)

Personnel:
Dave Brock: synthesizers, keyboards, guitars, vocals
Alan Davey: bass, vocals, synthesizer
Richard Chadwick: drums, percussion, vocals
Produced at Barking Dog Studios, Devon by Hawkwind, March-July 1993.
Highest chart place: 75 (UK)
Running Time (approximately): 63:17

'It Is The Business Of The Future To Be Dangerous' (Brock/Chadwick/Davey)

The title track starts the album with a disconcerting and discordant keyboard noise that sums up the album for long term fans. Taking a leaf from Ozric Tentacles the entire first half of the album (up to, and including, 'Wave Upon Wave') is entirely instrumental, save for deeply buried vocal samples. Ominous ambient space rock with Eastern music as its inspiration, the only true use for this is as background music for film and TV soundtracks. Swathes of synthesised sounds clutter up the ether while Chadwick produces an overly fussy and needlessly complicated drum rhythm, almost certainly using a drum machine.

'Space Is Their (Palestine)' (Brock)

The next three pieces are given political trappings with their controversial titles. The phrase 'Space is there' is extracted from a Calvert reading of Moorcock's 'The Black Corridor' and also punningly reworked into the title of this track, but its laboured wordplay reflects the monumentally over-stretched ambition of the track. Arabic-influenced music, it was welded on to live versions of 'Hassan I Sabbah' as a bridge and renamed 'Assassins Of Allah'. The music is expressive (and may well have influenced Nik Turner's 1994 Anubian Lights project) but far too much reliance is placed on sequencers and MIDI triggering of vast loops of sound. At eleven minutes it is entirely too long.

'Tibet Is Not China part 1' (Davey)

The suffocating synthesizers remain in place but at least there is the sound of human voices chanting (probably Tibetan) to give the piece a sense of identity.

The band are committed to the Free Tibet campaign and the original album featured the emblem for the campaign in the booklet.

'Tibet Is Not China part 2' (Brock/Chadwick/Davey)
Chadwick's drums don't really appear until this group jam, which sums up the whole album. Davey says this is the first take of an improvisation that followed the structured part 1. Carrying over the same chanting this, at least, has a recognisable trio sound that speeds up the tempo and reminds listeners that there is a band at play here.

'Let Barking Dogs Lie' (Brock/Chadwick/Davey)
Rather oddly starting with the sound of a truck being started, this uninspiring piece blunders around for a while before throwing in sampled dog barks. Brock lets his fingers wander over the guitar strings and Chadwick appears to have lost his drum kit as the cymbals get a sad tapping without contributing anything to the noise on offer. Nine minutes is far too long for this bland non-entity, even if it is inspired by the poor treatment suffered by traveller society.

'Wave Upon Wave' (Davey)
Aside from noting that the title describes the music perfectly, there is little of note from this ambient attempt to describe an acid trip.

'Letting In The Past' ['Looking In The Future'] (Brock)
The second half of the album contains the only songs that bear any relation to rock music, and here we have the initial example. Reusing Longfellow's opening stanza and revising a tune from *Church Of Hawkwind* this begins with a scattering of electronic drums and then proceeds at a jogger's pace to imitate a rock song. The tapping cymbals make their dubious reappearance, and the whole enterprise sounds somehow desperate as if the band know that they are muse-less and uninspired. The song actually extended further than the almost three minutes present here as the band played on.

'The Camera That Could Lie' (Brock)
Rolling directly on from the previous song, like a twisted middle eight, this relies upon an intriguing reggae groove and lifting lyrics from 'Living On A Knife Edge'. It is a daring direction for the band to pursue and one that should be regarded as a success, assuming that the listener enjoys dub reggae, as it reflects a large musical constituency of the free festival scene. Lamenting the rise of CCTV intrusion into everyday life, the current arguments around facial recognition use have only highlighted the issue presented here.

'3 Or 4 Erections In The Course Of A Night' (Brock/Davey)
This is titled after the vocal sample it uses although musically this is more of

the exploratory, and sometimes unmusical, instrumental textures. The speech comes from the 1984 film *Dreamscape* although its purpose is obscure. The whinnying horse sample from *The Chronicle of the Black Sword*-era makes a reappearance for no discernible reason, and the whole piece sounds like pointless filler.

'Techno Tropic Zone Exists' (Brock)

Heading for the final stretch, we are faced with Brock spouting verbal gibberish over a rhythm track that is too complicated and clunky for its own good.

'Gimme Shelter' (Jagger/Richards)

The album cut has Chadwick singing lead in order to blend it with the rest of the tracks. It doesn't work; the Brock-patented chunky guitar riff, superb harmonica (also from Brock) and passionate playing all contribute to the outstanding rock moment on the album. Dumping the iconic guitar riff and substituting a blazing new one is a brave move, especially as the band sample the opening seconds of the Rolling Stones original before spraying on that new riff. Chadwick's voice isn't strong enough to carry the verses or the bluntness of the words but the chorus multi-tracking of the vocals adds the requisite weight.

'Avante' (Brock/Chadwick/Davey)

Not before time, the end of the album is nigh, finishing with a combination of sweeping synthesizer, energetic drumming and, finally, the washes, bleeps, whooshes and electronica that has characterised the band since their inception. A brief simulated flute makes a welcome change but it disappears rapidly. This is the end six minutes, after fourteen minutes of improvisation, of 'Letting In The Past' from earlier on in the album. There is little to commend it to a listener unless they are in need of poorly realised background music.

Another double album release, this shows the law of diminishing returns for the band. Recorded around the same time as the 'Gimme Shelter' single, it marked the beginning of Davey's estrangement from the band (although he would participate in 1995's Psychedelic Warriors spin-off ambient techno album, *White Zone*, without protest). This album would have made more sense as another side project.

The album that most polarises fans, either loved or loathed, it betrays the band's desire to follow the current fashion of ambient techno space rock. An almost wholly instrumental, synthesizer and keyboard dominated ambient album it marks the final phase of technological integration for the band.

'Mists Of Meridin' (Brock/Davey)

A product of the same recording sessions, this was only released on an obscure American Church Of Hawkwind reissue as a bonus track. It features the trio line-up in mysterious mood with tinkling bells, drawkcab keyboards and a gently lilting pace that would have been a better choice for the album than a great deal of the dross that made it. Eschewing guitar, vocals and drums altogether, this gets closest to the ambient aspirations that the band were incorporating. Of course, it sticks out like a politician at a biker festival on the reissue that it graced, but there are ways to find it a good home now.

Touring Pains

After their third American tour in four years, the band were re-establishing themselves successfully. Attendances were up, Griffin Music were issuing albums in the U.S., and the band was looking forward to real success in the country. All that groundwork would be pulled from under their feet by a free-wheeling Nik Turner and American friends. Whether Turner knew about Hawkwind's American tours and capitalised upon it, or whether it was just an unfortunate coincidence, the band's plans were blown apart by a two-month coast to coast North American tour by the confrontationally named Nik Turner's Hawkwind. With a pickup American band of underground space rock luminaries, they were able to undercut Hawkwind's own fees. After injunctions and legal challenges, it was renamed Nik Turner's Space Ritual, an acceptable compromise that should have been obvious from the beginning. Unfortunately, Hawkwind would be unable to return to America for some years, because of this situation, and then the climate had changed so much that the invites would be to play single gigs as festival appearances rather than as a full touring proposition.

With legal bills looming Brock and Hawkwind suddenly found themselves without a record deal, unable to tour America (promoters were suddenly wary about booking them, not knowing which Hawkwind they would get) and reliant upon gigs and record sales in the UK to carry on. In a mind-bogglingly inept and naïve statement, Turner not only claimed that he had a perfect right to use the name (which is, perhaps, debatable) but also suggested that *everyone* who had ever been in the band could use the name too! Ginger Baker had tried it previously, but the idea that upwards of 50 Hawkwind's could be striding the live halls of the planet at any one time was not only unworkable but staggeringly impractical. The prospect of Dave Anderson's Hawkwind, Simon House's Hawkwind, even Lemmy's Hawkwind, and tens of others all trying to survive is astonishing although they, at least, have some claim to particular periods of the band's evolution. The thought that we could have Paul Hayles' Hawkwind (in the Sonic Assassins band and one tour as House's replacement but never appeared on a studio recording), Steve Bemand's Hawkwind (a one-time-only touring replacement for Brock in 1991) or Keith Hale's Hawkwind (a member of the band for about five months, although he did make it onto vinyl) highlights the absurdity of Turner's suggestion. Paul Hayles did, indeed, form the dubiously named Lastwind and is working with the reactivated Flicknife Records, while Harvey Bainbridge, Jerry Richards and, initially, Ron Tree have, they claim, reformed the Hawklords. Initially, they attracted Nik Turner and Alan Davey to their group but ended up with Adrian Shaw on several albums as well as guest appearances by Steve Swindells, Paul Hayles and Michael Moorcock before they slimmed down to a four-piece rock band. In their case, Brock desisted from resorting to the law and has allowed this prolific band to continue, albeit as a pale shadow of the original Hawklords.

The record label situation for Hawkwind was solved for the immediate future when their on-off manager, Doug Smith, instigated a label exclusively for the band, the Emergency Broadcast System, beginning their regime with another live album, The Business Trip. In 1994 the oft-delayed Ledge Of Darkness finally saw print, albeit in a way no-one could have predicted. Michael Butterworth had mapped out the basic plot, such as it was, and done some rough work on the script in 1978. Bob Walker was working as an artist for Hawkwind, beginning in 1985, and saw an opportunity to create his own graphic novel by adapting Butterworth's initial plot into a lysergic and hallucinatory underground comic. It took him more than five years and, in the end, he had to wait further years to find a publisher. It eventually came out as a very limited edition softback book that only ever accompanied the impressive 25th Anniversary four-CD compilation 25 Years On from American company Griffin Records. Ledge Of Darkness has never been reprinted, unfortunately, as it is an artistic tour-de-force that is one of the few pieces of illustration that even remotely conjures up an acid trip and the story even has its own internal logic and just about makes sense. There are some lovely asides and neat references, and the whole thing would have made a scintillating concept album (although very few people would have understood a word of it). Instead, the band pushed forward with a different idea.

Alien 4 (Emergency Broadcast System, October 1995)

Personnel:
Dave Brock: vocals, guitar, keyboards, synthesizers
Alan Davey: bass, vocals, synthesizer
Richard Chadwick: drums, percussion
Ron Tree: vocals
Jerry Richards: guitar
Produced at Earth Studio, Devon by Dave Brock, Alan Davey and Paul Cobbold, May-July 1995.
Running Time (approximately): 63:00

'Abducted' (Brock/Ron Tree)

Opening extremely strongly with this terrifying trip through Tree's alien abduction nightmares, accompanied only by the deep throbs and ominous rumbles of Brock's synthesizers and his prickly guitar scrapes, this augurs well for the rest of the album.

'Alien (I Am)' (Brock)

Brock then builds up the tension with this superb song, rocking out to fine effect. Integrating a sample from *Star Trek: The Next Generation* into the fabric of the concept is a touch of inspiration that, sadly, needed to be repeated elsewhere. Tree's voice is treated to all sorts of effects to create a dislocation from the usual human sound, although it cannot quite get away from the uncharitable thought that Tree merely chugged a balloon full of helium every time he emoted his vocal parts. Brock, meanwhile, sings in his usual style with the lyrics portraying an emotionless being that, therefore, lacks a soul. Implying that this applies equally well to aliens and humans, the protagonist laments their inability to feel. Based around a heavy and spirited guitar riff, and yet being backed by the techno sequencers and limp drum sound of previous albums, this is another case of almost-but-not-quite.

'Reject Your Human Touch' (Brock/Chadwick/Davey/Tree)

A synth bass and electronic drum splash are quickly submerged by Brock's forceful guitar work on this short linking piece which illustrates the title but little else.

'Blue Skin' ['I Am The Eye That Looks Within'] (Brock/Chadwick/Davey/Tree)

There are a lot more words on this album than recently, and this ranting exhibit is no exception. Tree continues his exploration of the dark side of alien lore on this striking conceptual piece, along with Brock's disturbing musings midway, all based on a previous piece of music that had been recorded for the previous album but never used. It features an unsettling guitar motif that punctuates the song intermittently and gives off an air of menace that permeates the whole album. 'I Am the Eye That Looks Within' is obviously a leftover from *It Is the Business of the Future to Be Dangerous*. It's long, largely instrumental, electronic and a little too padded for its own good. On *Alien 4* it has been truncated, remodelled and given a healthy lyrical overdose and resulted in something unexpectedly impressive.

'Beam Me Up' (Tree)

Tree and Davey are undoubted fans of *Star Trek* and this is made explicit here. The return to the Enterprise command is used as a refrain and sits atop a solid bass and drums rock song. Tree uses his alien voice again although his nuclear catastrophe speech is spoken in an anxiety-filled voice. This adds to the tension, but there is never a point at which this leaps from workmanlike to inspired.

'Vega' (Davey)

Another of Davey's interminable attempts at recapturing the magic of 'Realms' (he has several solo albums to his name that try to do just that), this instrumental slides along on tidal keyboards and spacey synths without arriving anywhere substantial.

'Xenomorph' (Davey/Tree)

Taking us back into the borderlands of the ill-focused concept this is a mid-paced rocker with Tree in rough-voiced Calvert territory, although his range is a little wider. Leaving out a lot of the synthesizer excesses and concentrating on the guitar, bass, drums triumvirate pays dividends on a chugging effort that captures an older Hawkwind spark. Breaking the word down, 'xenomorph' appears to mean that the alien is able to take on the physical characteristics of another species, in this case, humans. Lyrically, it's difficult to glean what Tree is ultimately talking about, even though he sings passionately. The tour programme provided a clearer explanation, saying this is 'an alien in his bloodshape, germinating and infesting like a virus', but not really giving any indication as to what this actually means in terms of plot or story.

'Journey' (Brock)

Another pedestrian linking piece, at least with a rock band line-up rather than the ambient textures so beloved of the band, this feels like a song waiting for words.

'Sputnik Stan' (Davey)

Placing such an outstanding song this late in the album really invigorates proceedings. A punky backing accentuates the thrills of this amusing scrap-merchant-in-space tale. The lyrics are based on the fact that there are several hundred tons of space junk circling the Earth, even in the present day, including antiquated satellites that are no longer working, a vast quantity of waste from the various space stations that are in orbit and the original Russian Sputnik spacecraft. Sputnik 1 ceased functioning decades ago, its only purpose was to broadcast a single repeating signal, while Sputnik 2 has a dead dog on board, Laika, the first living being to be sent into space. Liberally sprinkled with authentic space beeps, the song strides along very successfully, although Davey's vocals are a little blurred in the mix.

'Kapal' (Brock/Chadwick/Davey)

This feels like another linking piece, but it effectively ends the album in a spate of fluttering keyboards, half-formed rock riffs and curious space noises, some of which are again sourced from *Star Trek*. The final five songs (coincidentally featuring Jerry Richards' first recordings with the band) sound like a separate EP from a different project.

'Festivals' (Brock/Tait)

Originally adorning the rear cover of 1991's *Palace Springs*, Tait's heartfelt poem was set to a pounding rock beat with a glorious Brock tune which misses the melancholy of the lyrics but makes the anger very apparent. The words lament the final destruction of the free festival scene in 1990 which stemmed from a particularly nasty and brutal riot that occurred at one festival where Hawkwind were present, but which came from within the community itself rather than from any agent provocateur influence. Indirectly this situation was the catalyst that inspired Dave and Kris to initiate the Hawkfests that went on for many years.

'Wastelands' (Brock)

An entirely superfluous instrumental version of 'Wastelands of Sleep' was recorded for this album. Without the words, it is a pale shadow of its former self.

'Are You Losing Your Mind?' (Brock/Chadwick/Davey/Tree)

Surprisingly this would have fitted onto the main album as it seems to fit the concept pretty well, with Tree yelling at everyone who will listen that he has 'a silicon chip in my head' which is apparently controlling his mind. Short and sweet and rhythm-heavy this makes its point and leaves, much like the rest of the album should have done.

'Space Sex' (Brock)

This bonus track is a far better addition to the album, being a tight but fast song which has a lot in common with the conceptual part of the album. If 'Sputnik Stan' is *Steptoe and Son*-in-space, then 'Space Sex' is *Barbarella*, complete with kinky costumes and a rock and roll heartbeat although it fades out a little too soon, suggesting that it was an afterthought.

Ron Tree slotted easily into the trio although he found himself contributing to an album that had already been written and was in the early stages of recording. Adding lyrics, spoken word pieces and small pieces of music to make as much of an impression as he could, Ron also helped to conceptualise the album, although it still feels like a record that's not quite finished. The album hangs together with the themes of alien abduction, paranoia, conspiracy theory and mutation but never makes the leap from concept to classic narrative. Every song suffers from the soft drum textures that haunt the 1990s albums. Chadwick is an excellent drummer, but sometimes the digital studio drums sound woolly and damp when they should sound bright and crisp. If the band intended it to sound this way it is a mistake. Particularly on the rock songs, the punchier drum sound would only add to the weight of the music.

'Photo Encounter' (Brock)

Inevitably the commemorative double live album, *Love in Space*, contains new music but, disappointingly, two of the three pieces are merely instrumental keyboard washes, this being one of them. It pulses along ineffectually before it fades out altogether, in time for some astronaut chatter to briefly surface and then disperse.

'Love In Space' (Brock)

The only new song is a triumph that lifts this album above its' studio predecessor. A tranquil and emotive nine-minute ode to longing it eclipses everything else and confirms that Brock's songwriting muse hadn't entirely departed. Brock includes some nice lyrical touches in homage to Calvert:

> Drifting in our capsules of icy mist
> The ship of dreams sails on

and carries the song forward with his passionate vocals. The recording is a little poor and clearly there have been no overdubs as the whole ambience is unequivocally live with the drums sounding tinny and lacking in force. Nevertheless, this is a great addition to the concept and a boon to the studio album preceding it. Brock returns to the song on several occasions in the following years: an anaemic and shortened instrumental version pops up on *Distant Horizons,* but that only lays the groundwork for the 1998 wholesale rearrangement of the song that appears as a bonus track on the *Love In Space* reissue. Given a production makeover by Zeus B. Held, this appears to be an attempt to turn a slow-burning epic into a commercial techno-pop single, and it probably succeeds because it sounds bloody awful.

'Elfin' (Davey)

Davey gets to indulge his keyboard washes again with this disappointing retread of past ideas. It barely passes muster on a live album with several weaknesses already visible.

What Happened Next

The presence of a frontman allowed the band to shine again and the live shows were ecstatically received, particularly upon the production of Tree's homemade robot figure. Tree built it before he knew he was going to join the band, astonishingly. Almost immediately the Emergency Broadcast System added to Hawkwind's bid for current fashionability: in July 1996 an album of horrific, startling and, occasionally, excellent remixes appeared called *Future Reconstructions: Ritual Of The Solstice*. Aligning itself with several well known and respected dance remixers (Salt Tank, Utah Saints, Astralasia, Zion Train, etc.), it attempted to place Hawkwind within the ambient and dance floor context. To my mind, its only saving grace is a respectful and tasteful update of 'Uncle Sam's On Mars'. Otherwise, it's proof positive that people shouldn't get involved in remixes. It should come as no surprise to anyone that *Future Reconstructions: Ritual Of The Solstice* is not reviewed in this book.

In December 1996, Davey, having had enough of the mediocre guitar of Jerry

Richards (he had apparently nicknamed him 'Huw Lloyd Hillage' because of the perceived lack of his own playing identity) and smarting at the rejection of some of his new rockier songs, left the group to pursue his own band's fortunes.

Distant Horizons (Emergency Broadcast System, November 1997)

Personnel:
Dave Brock: vocals, guitar, keyboards, synthesizer
Richard Chadwick: drums, percussion
Ron Tree: vocals, bass
Jerry Richards: guitar, keyboards
Captain Rizz: vocals
Steve Smith: synthesizer
Produced at Earth Studios, Devon by Hawkwind, April-July 1997.
Running Time (approximately): 51:33

'Distant Horizons' (Brock/Chadwick)

Even with serious psi powers, nothing can prepare you for the jarring opening minutes of this wholly unexpected song. Most people will wonder if they have bought the correct album, such is the disconcerting noise on display. A blip of keyboards and studio chatter is swept away by a thumping drum and bass rhythm and the inane babbling and jabbering of Captain Rizz then intrudes. After almost three minutes of this abomination, a female voice cries out something about 'desire' (as if they are about to divert into pounding trance/dance) and then Brock's guitar finally cuts in and smears itself all over the uncalled for techno excursion that follows. Taking in some radical dance music influences (after the apparently perceived success (!) of the remix album) and clambering on to the several-years-out-of-date trance 'zeitgeist', this tragic exploration of new sounds and innovative intentions leaves the listener with the distinct impression that several old farts have been downloading their children's music and are trying to rebuild their own sound for this new generation. Both crass and horrific this is a blight on the album, and one cannot help wondering if this was why they never recorded anything else for the label.

'Phetamine Street' (Chadwick/Jerry Richards/Tree)

Richards obviously rummaged around Brock's farm studio as he turned up what appears to be an original audio generator which he immediately deploys here. A leaden and punky predecessor to Queens Of The Stone Age's vibrant 'Feel Good Hit Of The Summer' this thudding bass and drums led ode to club drugs and come-down pharmaceuticals ('phetamine, methedrine, ketamine') paints a poor picture of the state of Tree's health at this point as he questions the chemicals' effects on his dreams and on his future. Tree would later depart from Hawkwind in a haze of heroin addiction and would repeat his departure from the Hawklords over a decade later.

'Waimea Canyon Drive' (Brock)

Finally, a song that sounds like Hawkwind, or, at least, a reasonable solo Brock facsimile. A chugging guitar riff and a walking pace bass drum contribute to this evocation of a particularly beautiful drive that Brock and Tait took on their Hawaiian holiday, to Waimea Canyon, in fact. The music doesn't catch the wonder or exhilaration of this mini-Grand Canyon, and the lyrics are, in large part, just the title repeated over and over again. Pleasant listening and the best of the bunch so far, but hardly even a minor return to form.

'Alchemy' (Chadwick/Richards)

Starting with a raw and rocky Richards riff, this quickly degenerates into a repetitious trawl which would serve as a fine middle to another song but doesn't deserve its prominent independent placing here. Throwing in random voice-affected samples, does no favours to an already-confused song, and that remarkable riff really needs to be the anchor point for a far greater song, not just the instrumental thrashing about that it winds up with here.

'Clouded Vision' (Brock)

Another solo Brock piece, in all but name, this is a keyboard-based ballad of regret and nostalgia with a nice vocal and a delicate tune. It would be the highlight of a solo album but it gets rather lost in the sound and fury of the surrounding songs, albeit that they signify nothing in the end. A dual solo and riff provide a rough counterpoint to the almost cocktail lounge keyboards and Brock cuts the song off before it becomes unwelcome.

'Reptoid Vision' (Chadwick/Richards/Tree)

A deep and punky Tree bass and Richards' guitar hold this sharply contrasting song together. As if the band sequenced the album for slow/fast, quiet/loud, here is the thrusting rock piece to juxtapose with the calm of the previous song. Tree shrieks about his current obsession (the coming human/alien hybrid race that resemble reptiles) while forgetting to add a vocal melody or a decent chorus. Another of the trio recorded pieces, this has little time for keyboards and only just enough time for an astronaut's message in the middle eight before a Tree rant buries everything except for an atonal guitar. Repeating the opening verse with an ever more frantic backing is hardly endearing after masochistically subjecting yourself to the rest of the track.

'Population Overload' (Brock/Chadwick)

This is a rather disconcerting harangue from Brock on the dangers of overpopulation which is designed to act as a warning but lacks any clear thesis and certainly isn't about to proselytise a solution to this, inarguably genuine, problem. Putting the concerns to another plinky-plonky keyboard and drum machine backing is hardly likely to raise awareness either. Brock betrays the demo-like status of this song with the sudden sonic changes that perforate the piece. Tree attempts a rough-voiced rap intermission but this only sums up the disjointed and unsympathetic nature of the whole album. Stretching out the rhythmic sections into a semi-dub reggae beat and then closing with a brief Hawkwind trademark synthesizer only serves to show the schizophrenic heart of this song.

'Wheels' (Chadwick/Richards)

Purporting to be an environmentally aware spoken-word piece about the hugely negative effects of car culture, this is a fair piece of commentary, incongruously intoned by Brock who isn't even listed as one of the writers. As a touring rock band, however, using giant diesel trucks to haul their equipment from show to show, this could be seen, at best, as worryingly hypocritical. Musically the band offer us the now standard punky thrash with a strong riff, sturdy bass and lashings of the space rock approved audio generators which give a sense of the band as they should be but without any of the hooks that have always been a feature of their songs.

'Kauai' (Brock)

The rolling waves that start this piece were probably recorded on location on Kauai, a tropical island within the Hawaiian archipelago, where Brock and Tait went for an, obviously memorable, holiday. Again we return to the ambient synthesizers and tranquil pace of previous pieces that seek to evoke this paradise isle. The bonus alternate take adds an entirely spurious rhythmic-trance introduction that only goes to show that not every decision made about which takes to use for the album were the wrong ones.

'Taxi For Max' (Brock)

Clunks, whistles, silly noises and clanging metal make up this, mercifully brief, piece of musique concrete which has no redeeming features and no apparent relation to its title. Moving on…

'Archaic' (Chadwick/Richards/Tree)

Although credited to Brock, this is clearly the Tree trio ploughing their way through another generic piece of sturm-and-drang that is under-produced and blunt. Annoyingly misspelt on the cover, this bonus track has a scorching guitar riff but a bored-sounding vocal and flails about to little purpose. Lyrically the song looks at the wisdom that comes with experience. Tree sings 'archaic, archaos' as a short refrain, referencing the popular and anarchic Circus Archaos of the 1990s which had more to do with human stunts, feats of endurance and pyromania than the traditional clowns, performing elephants and caged lions. French in origin, this was the pioneer of 'New Circus' and led directly to the spectacle of Cirque du Soleil and its imitators. Ironically, Nik Turner had been a musical director for Gerry Cottle's conventional Circus in an earlier time. Turner, along with Davey, would end up working with Tree in the early stages of the Hawklords reactivation.

'Morpheus' (Brock)

Far more representative of this era of Brock music, this has a clattering opening rhythm that pops up throughout and a wailing series of inimitable guitar riffs and solos that give the track a sense of identity lacking in the bulk of the album proper. Giving both his higher-pitched and whispered vocal singing, Brock ponders, in its brief run time, on the nature and purpose of dreams. Morpheus is also known as the Sandman, master of dreams, and is both the subject of an acclaimed comic series by renowned author Neil Gaiman and a song by Metallica.

Jerry Richards gained 'man of the match' award for this album. Recording, engineering, programming, splicing and overdubbing were only part of his contribution. He frequently stayed late, and overnight, to complete mixes or finish off musical parts. He was instrumental in getting the album finished...

So it's a shame that the end result was so poor. The late 1990s were the worst time ever for Hawkwind. They reached a commercial nadir with this album and the slump in their fortunes that it created stumbled on for almost ten years. Nothing here is memorable, there's no conceptual link that unifies the album and the biggest criticism that you can lay at its door is that the songs are as bland as the cover. The grey of that disappointment hints at the empty grey tones of the music inside. *Distant Horizons* was the suggested title of the second Psychedelic Warriors album which was never released. That in itself should set alarm bells ringing. Some of the music destined for it apparently ended up here.

Witnessing the tour for this album was a painful experience, what with the low turn-out and sense of desperation. The group try toasting (a form of reggae rap which is as desperate as it sounds) with Captain Rizz, they take a second stab at the space reggae experiments first attempted in 1990, they try a thrashy sort of punk rock (the Tree, Richards, Chadwick songs) and they revert back to humdrum electronica when they can't find a better route. *In Your Area* was the ghastly odds and sods live/studio result.

'Rat Race' (Brock/Rizz)

This flabby live bridge section unceremoniously crashes into a twee version of 'Love In Space' after a minute or so. Brock plays well, but the jabbering Rizz detracts from proceedings, and the production is adequate without being punchy. The words are a reminder that we should join the human race rather than living in the rat race. Rizz does, at least, cater to his audience by suggesting that:

Everybody wants to live up on Mars
But you can't even live in your own universe

Disengaging, 'Love In Space' returns for the final few moments.

'I Am The Reptoid' (Brock/Chadwick/Richards/Tree)

Following Tree's 'Reptoid Vision' paranoid monologue from the previous album this is a further extrapolation on the same theme where, it seems, Tree is now terrified that he is one of the alien/human hybrids. Starting with a spoken word piece that details a fractured mind, Tree has time to indulge in some disturbing word mangling where he collides terms to come up with a new combined expression. He gradually starts to sing in a repeated refrain while speaking his newly coined words:

Invicerate
Thermetically

Musically, this is the undercarriage of 'Alien (I Am)' without the pulsing rock element and it barely gets going before it is sideswiped by the next, studio, track.

'The Nazca' (Brock)

This is a half-formed solo Brock idea that needs fleshing out, and not just from the female recitation that appears. The title refers to the giant, man-made, ancient artworks that adorn hills and plains in Peru that can only be appreciated when seen from the air. This has created a large body of speculative UFO lore that suggests it was made to communicate with intelligent aliens visiting the Earth. The speech implies that intelligent aliens must exist, otherwise the universe has no meaning.

'Hippy' (Chadwick/Richards/Tree)

The studio material consists of the odd interesting moment, and this is an example. It has a resounding rock vibe and a committed Tree vocal (or perhaps Richards sings lead here, judging from his recent Hawklords recordings) although, again, it is clear that Tree, Richards and Chadwick recorded their own material separately and are the only featured players here. It lacks much of the keyboard and synthesizer accompaniment that is usual for Hawkwind, but it stands on its own nevertheless. Confusing the term 'hippy' (a person with wide hips) and 'hippie' (a pejorative word used by hipsters to describe nouveaux pretenders) is an unexpected faux pas from people who should really know better. Setting the lyrics firmly in the Indian subcontinent and providing musical cues that echo similar use by Kula Shaker is a smart move and one that seems to predict one strand of the revitalised Hawklords songs that began a decade later.

'Prairie' (Chadwick/Richards/Tree)
A pretty guitar and synthesised harp instrumental that chimes along nicely but sounds out of place on a Hawkwind album as it bears a closer resemblance to laid-back Steve Howe or even Huw Lloyd Langton in contemplative mood. Although credited to the trio it is hard to identify Tree's contribution here and Chadwick only provides simple and unobtrusive percussion.

'Your Fantasy' (Brock/Chadwick/Richards/Rizz/Tree)
This is a Rizz-dominated train wreck that simply jams together several keyboard motifs from different songs and attempts to construct a drum and bass groove without having a strong drum sound or any idea of where to go. Rizz toasts over the top with little result and a lack of sympathy with the Hawkwind paradigm. Embarrassing is the kindest description. Dreadful is more accurate.

'Luxotica' (Brock/Chadwick/Richards/Tree)
Named after a Canadian company that supplies equipment for fire eating and fire dancing, this has probably come from Tait's background as one of the fire eaters and twirlers who regularly perform on stage with the band. Too disjointed for its own good, it sounds like the four members of the group added their contributions without listening to what had already been put on tape. Random keyboard chords, clattering percussion, a synthesised bass, guitar interjections and some jumbled voices as an introduction all add up to the bare hint of a tune. It would be a health and safety nightmare watching someone fire-eating to this atonal experiment.

'Diana Park' (Brock)
This is a Brock solo piece that, it is said, was inspired by Princess Diana. It has a programmed rhythm track and Brock layering soft lead guitar and synthesizers over the top which is, at least, a gentle end to another disappointing set of songs but, as with other contemporaneous songs, it carries on for far too long. Points for the trip-hop/ambient trance vein but this is clearly looking for a solo album rather than justifying its placement here on a Hawkwind album.

Conclusion

This is the final death rattle of Hawkwind before Brock again took hold of the reins and established some order.

7: War of the Hawks (1999-2006)

The unexpected and astonishing success of 1999's *Epocheclipse* collections and the financial marketing muscle wielded by EMI in their support, gave the band a new lease of life and a heightened profile in both the media and the wider world. The band finally started getting some of the recognition and acclaim they deserved. Unfortunately, the first concrete result of this was the disastrous Hawkestra gig of 2000 that featured practically every ex-member of the band but which ended up in chaos, lawsuits, live recordings under legal lock and key and a wealth of grumpy old men whingeing about the organisation, the band and the two camps that Hawkwind had split into. This farrago lead, in short order, to the forming of the rival xHawkwind (lead by Nik Turner and Dave Anderson) and the return of various guest artists to the current Hawkwind in the sporadic touring that followed. The lawsuit surrounding xHawkwind and its eventual, costly, mutation into Space Ritual (a perfectly sensible and obvious name for the band, and previously used in America, it is sad that it hadn't been resurrected in the first place) curtailed any recording activity for Hawkwind for a long time.

The concomitant desertion of Brock's songwriting muse after the bruising lawsuits and slanging matches meant that the only albums to appear under the Hawkwind banner for the next few years were either a dressed-up Brock solo album, *Spacebrock* (2000), or a series of contemporary live albums (*Yule Ritual* (2001), *Canterbury Fayre 2001* (2002) and *Spaced Out In London* (2004)) that generated a little money in order to ensure the band's survival. It would be eight years before Hawkwind released their next proper studio album...

By the time the band recommenced large scale touring in 2004/2005 several new songs were in the set. The band utilised Peter Pracownik painted backdrops, *Metropolis*-inspired statues, the inevitable projections, lights and lasers and still found room for costumed dancers, stage outfits and props for various songs. A new vitality seemed to infuse the band. New vigour, new purpose and new coverage from newspapers and television all combined to create an air of expectation and excitement around the new songs.

Then the media-friendly album appeared.

Take Me To Your Leader (Hawk Records/Voiceprint, September 2005)

Personnel:
Dave Brock: vocals, guitar, keyboards, synthesizers
Alan Davey: bass, vocals, keyboards, synthesizers
Richard Chadwick: drums, percussion, vocals
Jason Stuart: keyboards
Simon House: keyboards, violin
Jez Huggett: saxophone, flute, trumpet
James Clemas: organ

Arthur Brown: vocals
Matthew Wright: vocals
Lene Lovich: vocals
Produced at Barkalot Studios, Devon by Dave Brock and Alan Davey, August 2003-June 2005.
Running Time (approximately): 50:00

'Spirit Of The Age' (Brock/Calvert)
Re-recording this seminal song and stunt casting liberal TV motormouth Matthew Wright as a special guest star, could be seen as desperation or trading upon old glories. Davey suggests that it was due to the songs continuing relevance, but it's difficult to get away from the idea that this is an effort to cram in as many cameos and novelty ideas as possible. While a perfectly acceptable and, undoubtedly, well-produced version it has the bright and brittle production that is common with all digital recordings. Ten out of ten for getting to grips with the technology but, with hindsight, there needed to be more natural and random sounds and an analogue remix to really justify the lead-off song placement of this new version of an old classic. Wright performs his spoken piece well, although Brock does the actual singing, but the freshness and urgency are missing, even with a sterling new guitar line added.

'Out Here We Are' (Davey)
To seal Turner's fate forever, the band recruited noted jazz saxophonist Jez Huggett to guest on three tracks, and the result is a far more jazz-oriented set than ever before. This Davey tune suffers particularly. It may be old-fashioned, but Hawkwind have never really suited jazz. The upshot is a song that starts like classic Hawkwind, all big keyboards and atmospheric synthesizer use, but quickly reverts to aimless wandering. A nice little acoustic guitar figure is blasted out of place by the jazz saxophone that is plastered all over this cruising ambient instrumental.

'Greenback Massacre' (Davey)
Davey redeems himself, slightly, with this weightier rock song that explores the downside of monetarism in an aggressive form. The busily prominent bass is a little too upfront and the drum and bass opening salvo is incongruous, but it is the prosaic underlying keyboards and the deterioration in Davey's voice that are most noticeable, along with the continuing use of trance and techno influences. The chorus is barely visible from the surrounding verses, and that pretty much sums up this under-arranged song.

'To Love A Machine' (Brock)
When the best lyrical contributions are simply variations on a theme of 'Spirit Of The Age' it can't be avoided: Hawkwind have finally been reduced to

retreading past work. Turning the viewpoint around so that it is a woman who is the protagonist is hardly a radical gesture in these rather more enlightened times. Brock's sole solo songwriting contribution is the first really committed rock song of the bunch, and it almost makes up for the déjà vu moment of the lyrics. Incorporating the same delicate acoustic guitar sound heard before is a nice touch that almost binds the tracks together with some hint of a musical direction, although the song runs out of steam in the middle eight and Brock finds himself over-repeating the chorus. The lounge bar piano from Stuart that almost finishes the song is a mistake and makes very little sense in the context of the track itself.

'Take Me To Your Leader' (Brock/Chadwick/Davey)

The Hawkwind trio of *Electric Tepee* returns, and they steam along on this electro-dance monster that startles the listener with its further use of techno drum and bass almost entirely integrated into the Hawkwind bedrock. Brock intones a poetic but obscure verse while Chadwick sings about the power of music, although sadly this is just not enough to fill the entire album. The innovation on display is to be applauded, but it sounds incongruous, at best, in the hands of seasoned musicians. Chadwick had a decade-long appreciation of techno, hip-hop and dance music and this is obviously his influence at work here; with its swirling keyboard figures, sequenced cycling synthesizers and entirely artificial rhythm generation it couldn't be anyone else.

'Digital Nation' (Chadwick)

Here, Chadwick looks at the addictive downside of online gaming (from personal experience, it seems) where:

> I met so many friends there
> On this groovy secret level
> Where it's full-on artificial
> Intelligence heaven

He sings well, given the wordy nature of his lyrics, and allows room for tasty flute embellishments which enhance the low-key rock backing. Opening out, after a short voice sample, Brock makes a brief guitar cameo before the song resets itself and then carries on to its appropriately digital cut-off, accompanied by the reassuringly natural analogue flurries of flute.

'Sunray' (Arthur Brown/Davey)

Only the input of Arthur Brown turns up something exciting in the mix. Davey asked Brown to write lyrics about the joy his girlfriend brings him, as a ray of sunshine in his life. Glaringly owing a huge debt to Bowie's 'Heroes' this even has Bowie (and Hawkwind) alumnus Simon House contributing terrific violin parts to a cantering rock song that benefits from Brown's multi-octave range and a decent chorus. Quite why it needs an organ solo is a bit of a mystery, although it does provide a melodic counterpoint to Brown's screeching cries that signal the approaching end of this short but effective song. The striking guitar texture that finishes the song could only have been created digitally but is none the worse for that.

'Sighs' (Brock/Davey)

A short spoken-word piece with delusions, this is another quirky homage to the inspiration of *Church Of Hawkwind*, complete with drum machines and eclectic keyboard noises.

'Angela Android' (Brock/Chadwick)

Another lyrical variation on 'Spirit Of The Age' template (and without the profundity of the subtext) this suffers from a surprisingly puerile and misogynistic stance that starts from the very first words:

> Angela Android c'mon and be my babe
> I'm feeling horny and I want to get laid

There is little need to go on as it carries on in the same vein throughout. It is neither humorous nor interesting and it merely serves to highlight a worryingly teenage boy mentality. Given the dictum that 'the singer wrote the words', Chadwick is the likely culprit for this silly song. Dressing it up with jazz saxophone and calling on eccentric experimental pop chanteuse Lene Lovich to sing the final two verses in a computer affected stutter (or her unnatural voice, it is hard to tell) has guest star shock value but adds little to the song, except to unconsciously provide a bizarre riposte to Gong's 'space whisper' voice of Gilli Smyth. House's contribution on keyboards is submerged in the general tumult of the song and his only writing credit, on the thematically acceptable 'Cyberspace', was left off the final tracklisting. Given the galumphing mid-tempo beat this has an identity problem as it attempts to exhibit, in musical form, the sexual gyrations of the titular android although it actually brings to mind the sound of air escaping from a punctured sex doll.

'A Letter To Robert' (Brock/Brown/Chadwick)

Brown also supplies the largely extemporised rant that makes up the lyrical content of this song. It flashes with the old wordplay, wit and controversy of Calvert although its' disturbingly misogynistic tone is unkind to his memory and yet in keeping with the later tone of this album. It is almost as if Brown is channelling Calvert back into the band which is ironic because his ghost seems to infuse most of the songs here. The music is a low-mixed gallop through techno-land while the spoken word vocals are left to fend for themselves in a sea of space rock swoops and swirls. It stands outside any previous work by the band, and that is solely down to Brown's peculiar verbal contribution and it is a genuinely bizarre ending, to an eclectic album supposedly designed to restore the band's commercial fortunes.

The tray inlay would have made for a more amusing cover, with certain artistic additions, as there is an inquisitive-looking rabbit staring at the alien. Add the words 'take me to your leader' (and the Hawkwind logo) and the band could have giggled themselves around the world!

Around 2002 Brock bought and had installed new studio equipment in order that recordings could be made in Brock's milking shed. Having got new computers, programs and sequencers the band then spent a year in research and development learning how to use them. Over a further period of two years, the band made recordings, scrapped them, accidentally erased performances, lost other recordings in the memory of the computer, recorded new songs, left off other songs, rebuilt them and, on occasion, taped recordings and improvisations live. This is the main reason the album was delayed for so long. Well, that and the year-long search for an interested record company.

What is truly startling is that the album is so unconfined. Hawkwind albums have always held together as albums; partly through subject matter, partly through repetition, sometimes through a core of songwriters and sometimes just through a cohesive sound. Not on this occasion. It's clear that the songs were recorded piecemeal over several years. There isn't even a tentative concept running through the album, just the idea that this is set in a space laboratory (hence the lab coats worn on tour and the setting for the video of the single) and the mangled attempts to rewrite a classic.

'The Reality Of Poverty' (Brock/Morley)

Recorded at the same sessions, this has similar production values and, indeed, a similar musical structure to 1990s 'Images' which is no bad thing. Adding in a Brown spoken word section early on and lyrically referring back to 'Population Overload', this is a stunning and lengthy restatement of the best that Hawkwind have to offer. There is little hint as to whether co-writer Morley wrote the words or some of the music but it is of little import. This is, pretty much, full-on pulsating Hawkwind for more than nine minutes. Aside from the inevitable techno intrusions, this is as solid as the band got in this era. Brock largely takes the verses and the speech acts almost as a surrogate chorus which is surprisingly innovative and certainly memorable. House makes his presence felt on this as he screeches and wails violin over the serious words and charging rock backing. This should definitely have been on *Take Me To Your Leader*.

What Happened Next

Sadly, the album didn't sell as well as had been hoped. The figures were a considerable improvement on the past five to ten years, but the commercial breakthrough that had been hoped for wasn't forthcoming. What it did do, however, was revitalise the live experience. This line-up of Hawkwind eased back on their heavy touring schedule, slightly, but still played at least one tour every year. The four-piece lineup of Brock, Davey, Chadwick and late addition Jason Stuart gelled into a fine live rock band: tight, energetic and sprightly. Eschewing the meandering electronic twists of old this was a band enjoying the live arena again and not looking for guest players to create the excitement. Each gig was an occasion, each encore a gift. And, for the first time, Davey's Motorhead fixation came to fruition. His bass playing *does* sound like Lemmy and his vocals are beginning to catch up with the razor-blade throated roar of the man himself. Additionally, the band ended their sets with a storming version of 'Motorhead' itself where Davey was to the fore. In June 2007 Davey made the decision to exit the band again, for good this time.

2007 was another year of passings but this time much more expected. Brock's mother died on 8 January, aged 94. His father died on 1 September, at a staggering 100 years old. It certainly bodes well for Brock's longevity! To counterbalance the passings Brock and Tait married, after almost twenty years of partnership, at the increasingly regular Hawkfest (which aimed to recreate the spirit of the old free festivals but with a tighter rein on security). For the annual Christmas gigs, the band unveiled their new singer/bass player, ex-Krel and Spacehead member Mr Dibs and the reintroduction of old friend Tim Blake. Brock takes on a lot of genuine lead guitar and Blake guests to an energetic degree, looking gleeful at the band's new lease of life. He and Brock trading Theremin solos is a wonderful sight to behold. Brock seemed to be re-invigorated by Stuart's presence and once again seemed cheerful and attentive on stage. The heartfelt and genuinely emotional response from Brock at Stuart's extremely unexpected death from a brain aneurysm in September 2008 was in stark contrast to the unwarranted perception of Brock as a greedy, selfish manipulator who lacks feeling and empathy. Brock, on the contrary, confounds the naysayers and shows himself to be touchingly human and humane.

For the December 2008 tour, another Hawkwind acolyte was called up for service. Niall Hone is known for his psychedelic guitar/synthesizer playing and proved to be a fine choice on the ensuing tour. His more freeform instrumental approach proved to be engaging for Hawkwind aficionados of old. This new line-up took its time to gel organically, rather than placing burdens upon themselves, but proved to be a prolific studio beast.

8: Hawkwind Ascendant (2007-2019)

Blood Of The Earth (Eastworld, June 2010)

Personnel:
Dave Brock: vocals, guitar, synthesizer, theremin
Tim Blake: keyboards, theremin, vocals
Mr Dibs: bass, vocals
Richard Chadwick: drums, vocals
Niall Hone: guitar, synthesizer
Matthew Wright: vocals
Jason Stuart: keyboards
Produced at Earth Studios, Devon by Hawkwind, February-December 2009 (except 'Starshine': 2006).
Running Time (approximately): 52:34

'Seahawks' (Brock)

Brock contributes only two songs, this somewhat pedestrian almost-instrumental and the later 'Comfy Chair', to proceedings. 'Seahawks' starts well with a self-referential sample and a dynamic opening and it pounds along reasonably, but it outstays its welcome by several minutes with a dire pomp rock keyboard solo taking the reins and then descending into a trudge that is just Hawkwind-by-numbers. Even though it is inspired by the forthright Sea Shepherd whale-saving charity, the piece itself lacks either inspiration or originality.

'Blood Of The Earth' (Brock/Matthew Wright)

Throwing in a tidal backing for Matthew Wright's brief environmental poem, Brock redeems himself slightly with some odd noises and vocal effects which illustrate the damage being done to the planet. The poem itself is inspired but too short. It feels like a piece stripped out from a longer section where it should have been a stirring polemic for ecological concerns.

'Wraith' (Blake/Chadwick/Jonathan Darbyshire/Niall Hone)

The rest of the album showcases the band's songwriting and, by and large, it is effective, especially this group-penned charge that is both a sturdy and fast-paced space-rock song which may lack musical hooks but embeds itself in the mind through repetition. The lyrical subject matter seems to be about animal spirits, which is certainly unique. Blake has tremendous fun with his guitar synthesizer, and the techno trappings and drum and bass rhythms of before are either absent or integrated so well that the song retains its essential space rock nature and the furious drumming that closes the track is clearly real rather than manipulated.

'Green Machine' (Hone)

This debut instrumental from Hone is a synthesizer and guitar heartbeat-paced piece that inspires confidence for his further contributions. It may be a tad long, some of the keyboard solos could have been left off, but it replaces similar Davey material from the past with aplomb.

'Inner Visions' (Blake)

Bucking against stereotype, Blake presents a song, complete with words, to the band and it is a strong one. Known for his melodic and ambient instrumental work, Blake has also written many songs and this contribution takes pride of place on the album. Utilising a battery of keyboards and sequencers and combining it with real drums, bass and guitars Blake creates a mid-tempo rock song with hints of a dance undercurrent. Singing in a voice that has aged into a whiskey-soaked gruffness, Blake may not have a wide range, but he can just about hold the tune. There is a whiff of Alan Davey in the vocals and more than a hint of cyberspace in the lyrics which places it, thematically, rather more with the previous album.

'Sweet Obsession' (Brock)

Following the staunch determination of 'Inner Vision' with this rocked-up remake of a decades-old solo Brock tune is an odd choice. Most fans will already know this song, even if it is tricked out in gaudy new guitar swatches and amphetamine-fuelled drums, and will be disappointed that the vocal melody remains exactly the same. Brock's singing has barely changed in 27 years, but the parping keyboard sounds are intrusive and unsettling. While the backing is a definite improvement on the original, it is indicative that Brock has lost his muse that he has recycled such an old song.

'Comfy Chair' (Brock)

Everyone can be forgiven for thinking the obvious here: this lilting song seems to encapsulate Brock's feelings of the time as if he wants to make it entirely plain that retirement is on his mind. Now, with hindsight, it is clear that Brock was suggesting a breather rather than a full stop. Using the same acoustic guitar tone as *Take Me To Your Leader* this warmly laid-back ode to happy relaxation is a gentle highpoint on a consistent album.

> S is for smiles, big ones, and small
> They sure bring sunshine to one and to all

is hardly great poetry but it sets the atmosphere of joy that permeates the song. There are lovely synthesised fiddle parts from Blake (imitating House at times) and a charming melody to latch on to.

'Prometheus' (Blake/Chadwick/Darbyshire/Hone)

A loping and slow-paced attempt at a genuine space-rock song this has Eastern-inspired keyboards and a crashing rhythm that mixes machine with man, much as the lyrics do. Dibs' vocals cannot quite do the choruses justice and so the end result is a solid but not spectacular entry in this quartet's songwriting folder. The fact that the words jumble up a great deal of astrophysics (gravity waveforms, neutron stars) and mental phenomena into a song that appears to be about the evolution to Homo Novus (new humans) or a new breed of superior humanity causes some head-scratching for interpretation.

'Sentinel' (Blake/Chadwick/Darbyshire/Hone)

The final example of the quartet at work, this is a deep cut that grows with each repetition. It has a slow-burning hook and a delicate melody over the crawling pace that suits the mood and lyrics. Obviously inspired by *2001: A Space Odyssey*, this is a tale of the moon monolith that stands guard patiently awaiting the return of life to Earth. Each musician contributes a little solo without being overbearing, and the net result is a genuinely haunting addition to Hawkwind's legacy.

'Starshine' (Brock/Jason Stuart)

In tribute to Stuart, Brock constructs an elegiac piece of music that stands somewhat outside the Hawkwind canon. Fluttering spacey sounds are everywhere but the aching guitar tells a more human tale of sadness, regret and loss. It is a lovely instrumental panegyric to a fallen comrade, and it says a lot about Brock's feelings at the time. Whether Stuart shone like a star while he was on Earth or whether he has joined the stars in space and is shining down upon the world, it is a beautiful image and a tune that Brock should be proud of.

'Sunship' (Darbyshire/Hone)

As a bonus track for vinyl, this didn't get a lot of coverage, but it deserves greater exposure. An almost acoustic folk-inspired bass and keyboards piece, Dibs sings in a plaintive echo that carries a sense of melancholy with it. The words are a little messy conceptually and awkward to interpret and, given that Dibs is proficient on the electric cello, it would have been a real delight to have heard it on this tune.

Conclusion

After an extremely well-received 40th anniversary tour, and the enforced line-up change, *Blood Of The Earth* is the first concrete evidence of the new band's direction. This is remarkable because they appear to be trying to emulate a much earlier version of their sound. The noise is thicker and fuller than recent work, although this could come from the compression placed over the album, which may have resulted in Dibs' curiously colourless vocals. Astonishingly maintaining the same line-up as the previous album, the band forged ahead with a double CD release less than two years later and more music was in the vaults for future use.

Onward (Eastworld, April 2012)

Personnel:
Dave Brock: vocals, guitar, keyboards, synthesizer, bass
Tim Blake: keyboards, synthesizer, bass, vocals
Mr Dibs: bass, vocals
Richard Chadwick: drums, vocals
Niall Hone: guitar, keyboards, synthesizer, bass, vocals
Jason Stuart: keyboards
Huw Lloyd Langton: guitar
Produced at Earth Studios, Devon by Hawkwind, 2008-2012.
Highest chart place: 75 (UK)
Running Time (approximately): 81:28

'Seasons' (Chadwick/Darbyshire/Hone)

Opening with this ferociously catchy assault on politicians, greed and the looming environmental crisis, the group forge ahead with confidence. The implication of the lyrics is that the seasons have started to disappear and are running out of step with the natural order. On a basic level, this affects all life on Earth and has the catastrophic consequence that famine and starvation will result. Chilling in outlook, this song has a strong commercial sheen and a provocative Dibs chorus, along with a sprawling guitar that spends much of the track soloing. Brock seemingly emulating the Lloyd Langton method by plastering guitar runs everywhere and even chucking in an actual solo to catch the listener.

'The Hills Have Ears' (Brock/Chadwick/Hone)

Cracking straight on with a second psychedelic rock song bodes well, although the strained Chadwick vocals are a letdown compared with the opener. The sharp crashes in rhythm suggest that Chadwick had a hand in the musical content as well. The quiet sections are warbling space synthesizers while the energetic verses are Hawkwind reinvigorated and sounding epic. Quite why the writer wants to remind the listener of the film *The Hills Have Eyes* is a curious question.

'Mind Cut' (Brock)

Possibly resulting from the acoustic sets by the band, Brock resurrected a space-drenched folk song about the joy of living outside in the countryside. Originally written in his earliest busking days, and known as 'Get Yourself Together', this sweet song also appears in live form on 2019's *Acoustic Daze*.

Here, real guitars are joined by real drums and Brock sings a lilting paean to the wonder of nature and the strange human predilection for war and conflict.

'System Check' (Blake/Brock/Chadwick/Darbyshire/Hone)
This starship flight deck chatter set to synthesised choirs features every band member with a short spoken part and an overwhelming sense of déjà vu: the live concert *At The BBC – 1972* features a piece called 'Countdown' which has numerous echoes here.

'Southern Cross' (Blake)
Part of a much longer solo track, 'On Contemplating The Southern Cross', this showcases Blake as ambient rhythm conductor with its rolling momentum and virtual lead guitar work played on a guitar synthesizer with the rest of the band contributing their inimitable musical personalities and Blake layering a melodic theremin sparkle on top. Naturally fading out, rather than going for a rock band exit, this has Blake's sure touch and the aspiration of recreating the feeling of seeing the actual Southern Cross in the sky above Australia (during a Hawkwind tour, no less).

'The Prophecy' (Brock)
Clattering in as a live-sounding 'captured' moment, yet with Brock singing in a forced upper register that lacks colour and expression, there is a sense of spontaneous exploration and musicians in sympathy with each other that is undermined by the sudden musical box intrusion of the ending. Brock turns his attention to Eastern philosophy here but never quite nails either the vocal melody or the lyrical substance.

'Electric Tears' (Brock)
This is a short interlude of drawkcab guitars and keyboards, which is essentially a bit of aural fluff to bump up the time.

'The Drive By' (Brock)
Altogether more substantial and focused, this sturdy instrumental has a steady rhythm section that wanders into Ozric Tentacles fusion territory and an eccentric attitude towards alternating lead instruments. Combined with the odd trance elements this ends the first half on an obscure trail.

'Computer Cowards' (Brock)
Splashing on the digitally re-created sound of an old 78RPM record, as backing for an Elton John styled piano introduction, is a brave left-field decision that is instantly undercut by the throbbing rock whisper that emerges. Brock adds extra verses and recycles the more scabrous lines from his *Agents Of Chaos* song 'Hades Deep':

Beware you slithering slime of Earth
You shall return to the time of birth
We shall destroy your civil globe
And slice apart your left earlobe

We'll melt your tongue after sealing to a knot
We'll melt you down to liquid snot
Your hair will burn from the acid rain
And we will then surgically remove your brain

Thereafter, he throws in random samples and sound effects (computer bleeps, jaw harp, kettles whistling, mooing cows, telephones ringing) to finish off a worthy addition to their rock song repertoire, even if the lyrics are potty.

'Howling Moon' (Brock)

There are definitely samples of howls here, but the overriding impression is that Brock is channelling Bainbridge in a bizarre synthesised face-off that scratches around with very little purpose for two minutes before thankfully fading out.

'The Flowering Of The Rose' (Blake/Brock/Chadwick/Darbyshire/Stuart)

Touted as a bonus track, this instrumental tribute to Stuart was initially released as a free download called 'Dam Jam Jason' from the band's website. It has a live bedrock from a 'Damnation Alley' improvisation (hence the name) but was subjected to a little studio tinkering to produce its final form here. Apart from distant Brock guitar figures, this could be a new song albeit with a similar pace to its predecessor. Stuart displays his dexterity on the keyboards without ever descending into pomp rock excess and the eight minutes fly past in a blur of technicolour excitement and atmosphere.

'Trans Air Trucking' (Blake/Brock)

Atonal keyboards, foghorns, telephone answering messages, horses whinnying and other samples scatter the air as Brock introduces another bouncy piece of electronica to the Hawkwind repertoire. Blake is the musical culprit for the bulk of the track, but Brock adds his askew vision to the mix.

'Deep Vents' (Brock)

Synthesised low-end chords and rippling space swooshes are the only noises heard here and, at 32 seconds, it is more than enough.

'We Two Are One' (Brock/Chadwick/Darbyshire/Hone)

Neither credited on the sleeve, nor in the booklet, this is a secret bonus track lurking unawares. Possessing an atmospheric live-in-the-studio feel, that contrasts with the indifferently recorded live material and the studio-crafted bulk of the album, there is a buttoned-down studio version available on the strange hybrid album Spacehawks. Perhaps the band noticed the relative lack of new rock songs and placed this work-in-progress beyond the disappointing 'Green Finned Demon' finale. If so, it works a treat. Punching in with a ferocious rhythm all the vocalists get a turn and the bass is well up in the mix, only the tinny ticking in the middle eight is slightly aggravating. It all finishes with the patented whirling, swooshing synthesizers that are so commonly deployed when ideas have dried up. The Spacehawks re-recording omits this ending and provides a suitably rock-band finish.

Conclusion

Again a mix of new songs and re-recordings of old material, this at least has the surfeit of material to produce a really superb single-disc album. Burying the bonus tracks in the middle of the second disc is an obscure decision that interrupts the flow just a little too much. The album itself appears to harp even further back into the band's history by producing a thick, syrupy, almost sludgy sound which comes from the compression used at the mastering stage. While working on this album, there were two further projects underway. Breaking the dam of his muse, Brock's fifth solo album *Looking For Love In The Lost Land Of Dreams*, appeared in 2012. Brock, Chadwick and Hone all live in Devon and, while the rest of the band were unavailable, this trio (dubbed the Hawkwind Light Orchestra) produced the third all-new album in a single year.

Stellar Variations (Esoteric Antenna/Cherry Red, November 2012)

Personnel:
Dave Brock: vocals, guitar, keyboard, synthesizer
Richard Chadwick: drums, vocals
Niall Hone: bass, guitar, keyboards
Produced at Earth Studios, Devon by Hawkwind Light Orchestra, 2011.
Running Time (approximately): 53:22

'Stellar Perspective' (Brock/Chadwick/Hone)

Opening with a decidedly modern heavy rock riff and treated Brock vocal this surges and swoops with all the Hawkwind panache of old. Chadwick sings in a higher register counterpoint impressively recalling the nasal whine of Perry Farrell (of Jane's Addiction fame), but still exhibiting the same electronic treatment to his voice, all the while drumming in a rather more ambitious dub-laden rhythm than recently. Hone gets to prove himself with his powerful bass playing and the only reasonable perspective on this song is that it is, indeed, stellar. Undoubtedly influenced by the film *Blade Runner*, this tale of androids breaking their programming to hide within the human population and escaping their enslavement is a stunning return to form for Hawkwind.

'All Our Dreams' (Brock)

Pretty keyboard bells and piano accompany this crooned psychedelic Brock ballad which diverts in its second half to an arty dreamscape of fizzing synthesizers and then morphs into a weird jazz-funk section that recalls nothing so much as Wham! with its synthesised horns and bouncing rhythm. Talk about absorbing new influences; this takes the biscuit (and probably the crumbs too).

'Damp Day In August' (Brock)

More of an evocation of the tides of space or the seashore than the title implies, this is no damp squib just a little vignette that prefigures the next grand statement.

'It's All Lies' (Brock)

The fiery and political Brock of old is unleashed on this stirring broadside against the media and the social state of the nation. While the chorus is merely workmanlike, the verses are able to bear the repetition that they are subjected to. The lull of the middle eight, where Brock indulges his Dave Gilmour guitar impression, is quickly dispensed with and then, in classic song tradition, the song recapitulates.

'Variation 3' (Brock)

A space-bass funk groove oozes around the semi-melodic keyboards in this trance instrumental that gets sideswiped by a sudden driving rhythm designed to wake up the complacent in its latter stages. The other two variations are nowhere to be seen.

'Four Legs Good, Two Legs Bad' (Brock/Chadwick/Hone)

Drawing its inspiration from George Orwell's novel 'Animal Farm', this techno-trance throb has another appearance by the whinnying horse sample but mostly relies on the title repeated as a hypnotic mantra. The remaining spoken lines are heavily distorted, sounding much like a monster from *Doctor Who*, which comment directly upon a world without the two legs. Underlying all this is a concern for animal welfare and, perhaps, an allusion to the path of veganism.

'In The Footsteps Of The Great One' (Brock)

Japanese-influenced synthesised koto music runs throughout this bizarre, practically spoken word, mash-up of the lyrics to 'Song Of The Swords' and 'Horn Of Fate' set to a droning synthesizer. Perhaps this is one experiment too far or just the latest in a long line of pointless rehashes. There are some intriguing moments and a sense of freshness to the sounds and influences at work here, but the end result is a poor piece that could have been stripped down for parts rather than up-scaled with second-hand lyrics.

'A Song For A New Age' (Blake)

Acknowledging their absent bandmate, it is rather sweet of the trio to cover an old Blake number. When it first appeared in 1978 it was a twee, and musically out of step, acoustic guitar and spacey synthesizers folk tale charting Blake's reawakening after his somewhat fraught departure from Gong and the soul-searching that resulted. The version the trio present here is altogether tougher and lacking in the folk base that made the original so divisive. Chadwick proffers a throatier vocal and the trio power up the chorus for a decidedly rockier rearrangement which does justice to the original but is in no danger of eclipsing it, especially with the raspy shouts that Chadwick ill-advisedly throws in. The spacey synthesizers, unsurprisingly, remain firmly and reassuringly in place. Blake was gracious, and perhaps politic, about the cover when he heard about it, although he departed from the band in 2012 before the album was released.

'We Serve Mankind' (Brock/Hone)

This techno-trance groove thunders along as if it has a club audience in mind, all the while sprinkling theremin and space swoops over the top in a vain effort to disguise its dance foundations. The fact that this in no way detracts from the tune illustrates the total integration of these newer sounds into the Hawkwind musical arsenal. Coupled with the surprisingly catchy pop chorus this lyrical variation on 'Stellar Perspective' has a good deal to say about a postulated android uprising. Slipping in references to Frank Herbert's *Dune* ('deserts of spice for you to taste') and online gaming ('battles fought which you control') the song is both instant and rewards repetition.

'Cities Of Rust' (Brock)

Brock muses on the ecological cataclysm that is upon us, reminding us with pessimistic seriousness that:

> No ships to the colonies
> No rockets into space
> What do you do with the leftovers?
> The dregs of the race

even though he puts in a mock pre-flight announcement from a pilot before hitting us with the whispered doom of the verses. This is clearly a Brock solo piece with its electro-rock sound and machine drums, but it packs a wallop in the midst of its synthetic haze.

'Instant Predictions' (Brock/Chadwick/Hone)

A mid-paced plodder, this has Chadwick getting wordy over the strong rock backing but it lacks a chorus for that final touch. Chadwick repeats the vocal melody for each verse so that it appears to have a musical consistency and then, as ever, it fades out in electronic waves. The words are incongruously optimistic, or at least sanguine, given the earlier pronouncements on the album:

> But the message that we're sending is the same
> Hope springs eternal in the heart of man and
> Music is a weapon of peace

These words sum up what the band continues to strive for.

To celebrate and promote the long-awaited *Warrior On The Edge Of Time* reissue Hawkwind then embarked on several mini-tours during the year and resolved to play the complete album, in order, as part of the set. Recalling Dead Fred to the fold for violin and keyboard duties, to round out the sound, the band played with surprising vigour and, in Richard Chadwick's case, with a spring and a weight to his drumming that had been lacking for some years in studio recordings. A place-holder compilation, *Spacehawks*, was issued in 2013 featuring disappointing *Warrior On The Edge Of Time* re-recordings and a smattering of new works:

'Sacrosanct' (Brock)

With restless frequency, Brock explores some, often best undiscovered, musical blind alleys that might be fodder for his more eclectic solo excursions but hardly deserves a place on a Hawkwind album. Stretching this keyboards and synthesizer jazz-dance curiosity for over 8 minutes borders on torture. Far from sacrosanct, this diabolical musical doodle ranges from irreverent to profane, mostly recalling Frank Zappa's instrumental 1980s excesses in a similar area. Contributing some vocals to this electro-jazz monstrosity might just improve it but placing this instrumental pudding inside a 'Master Of The Universe'/'Sentinel' sandwich does it no favours whatsoever.

'Touch' (Brock)

Recommended only by its brevity, this starts as a barely musical theremin and radio-tuning Brock idea that has a quirky attraction with its lightly plucked guitar chords and marimba-like fade, and it could work as a bridging piece to something else.

'The Chumps Are Jumping' (Brock)

That 'something else' is not this, however. A silly title adorns a sketched idea of a song that needs some tweaking but has possibilities. A great ascending build-up of synthesizers rushes along breathlessly as if it is about to explode into hard rock heaviness, but then it just fades and dissolves into an unsatisfying denouement.

'Lonely Moon' (Hone)

Remembering how to do Hawkwind ambient instrumentals, Hone delivers a deep space vibe while piling on the melodic urgency with the piano at the forefront.

The Machine Stops (Cherry Red Records, April 2016)

Personnel:
Dave Brock: vocals, guitar, keyboards, synthesizer
Mr Dibs: bass, vocals
Richard Chadwick: drums
Niall Hone: bass, keyboards, synthesizer
Dead Fred: keyboards, violin, vocals, guitar
Haz Wheaton: bass
Athene Roberts: guest violin
Produced at Earth Studios, Devon by Hawkwind, 2015-2016.
Highest chart place: 29 (UK)
Running Time (approximately): 58:29

Pausing only to regurgitate the entirety of *Space Ritual* with the then-current band (with a headline-grabbing appearance by Brian Blessed on 'Sonic Attack'), for one performance only, the group began working on their first conceptual opus for two decades. Confirming that his songwriting libido was in full flow, Brock released his sixth solo album, *Brockworld*, in 2015 that, astonishingly, had no re-recordings or updates of old music or lyrics at all.

E.M. Forster's 1909 short story 'The Machine Stops' is a remarkably prescient slice of speculative science fiction which posits that the human race will live underground after a devastating apocalypse has made the surface uninhabitable. Occupying their own little 'cells' people will only interact through their messaging machines, where they can see and be seen, and retreat from anything but a virtual life. Travel exists using air-ships, but they are seldom used. The titular machine of the title provides everyone with their food, clothing, entertainment and education. Some people inevitably start to worship the machine as an infallible deity, while others begin to question their existence within the machine world. If any of this sounds familiar, then you have spotted the reason Brock got excited by the thought of a concept album based on the story and its inherent relevance to today. It also helped that the story itself is out of copyright which means that no-one would baulk at any liberties the band might take with the story.

'All Hail The Machine' (Brock/Darbyshire)

This spoken scene-setting piece borrows liberally from its source material and presents the milieu of the album in glorious detail, all backed by machine-created music just to reinforce the message. Delicately suggesting the ultimate breakdown of the machine with its sly detuning moments, there is a, perhaps intentional, resemblance to the live musical backing to 'The Chronicle of the Black Sword' poem, Hawkwind's last great concept.

'The Machine' (Brock/Chadwick/Darbyshire)

The sound of alarms is briefly heard before this defiantly 'live' sounding rock beast clatters into life. Dibs takes the verses while Brock covers the harmonies and backing vocals, singing of the history of this culture and the desire of one person:

> Oh, to reach the surface once again
> And feel the sun!

There is an intricate repeated guitar figure from Brock and a great deal of genuine live drum sounds which add to the authenticity of the song, especially when they finish with a touching musical nod to the recently passed Lemmy in the form of a growling bass, King-heavy drums and the ubiquitous rhythm guitar of Brock wind up to a throbbing finale.

'Katie' (Brock)

In need of a tinkling instrumental, that illustrates the soothing music played in peoples cells? You won't find anything better than this. It slows gradually to leave just the sound of breathing. The title bears little relation to the music or story, however.

'King Of The World' (Brock)

With a jerky guitar motif and a tribal rhythm, this evocation of the desire to break free of the cloying habitat that the protagonist lives within is layered with ideas from 'primitive' spirituality:

> Each one would guide us
> Further towards the distant sun
> 'Cos Rama was the 7th
> When will the next one come?

Brock puts the lyrics of 2012's 'The Prophecy' to a new tune and maintains his strange obsession for the number 7. Rama is a Sanskrit name for a woman meaning 'lofty'.

'In My Room' (Brock)

Returning to the spacey keyboard sounds of old, Brock throws in a brief heavy rock section to sing of the closed environment of his cell where the hero dreams of evolution and revolution, then the sounds of the outside world intrude with rain and storms and deadened keyboards. These are either Machine-generated sounds or only in the mind.

'Thursday' (Brock)

A patented Pink Floyd slow beat rolls through this light rock confection which takes the story deeper, even into the subconscious. Although never named on the album, the original story is about a mother (Vashti, a Persian name meaning 'lovely') and her son (Kuno, a German epithet meaning 'honest advisor') who live in cells on opposite sides of the world. 'Thursday' is Vashti watching her life drift past her and momentarily despairing of the existence she leads. Kuno has asked her to fly by air-ship to him and Vashti has a momentary pause:

> See it as you really are
> Can I escape and lose myself?

Brock must have smiled when he penned those words.

'Synchronized Blue' (Brock)

A remarkably straight, riff-driven rock experience, this is Vashti discovering that the world is no longer scarred and barren but apparently green and fecund. She does not like this assault upon her world view and pleads with the Machine to mend her 'ill-informed' perception, although she is in the air-ship at the time and has no access to the Machine. Brock puts in a surprisingly nimble keyboard solo and a lovely musical hook that makes up for the wordy chorus:

> But what I find above the ground
> Cannot be exactly true
> I was told on the screen
> The ground was charred
> It was black, not green

'Hexagone' (Phillip Reeves)

Dead Fred gets a solo spot and produces a lilting synthesizer and drum machine ballad that explores Vashti's thoughts and feelings about her trip to see Kuno. Singing in an almost falsetto voice, Reeves echoes the lighter-than-air transport. The chorus fleshes out Vashti's world view:

> I've never seen the daytime
> I to the ground belong
> I always fear the Homeless
> My life is Hexagone.

All the underground living areas are hexagonal, Reeves making a nifty play on words as he implies that existence in these rooms is meaningless. Within the story, the threat of Homelessness is akin to death. The Machine makes people Homeless if they do not conform, although there are rumours that people live above ground voluntarily.

'Living On Earth' (Brock)

Based around Brock's treated vocals, wordy lyrics and a lightweight rock backing, which has a startling country music break complete with fiddle and banjo dropped in, this is realism intruding upon fantasy:

> I didn't know, no-one told me of this
> That living on Earth is no life of bliss

'The Harmonic Hall' (Hone)

Another solo spot, this time with Hone in charge, inevitably it starts with a gong being struck and then tears into a musically modern ambient trance instrumental. Melodically rich in Eastern tones but obscure in narrative purpose, Hone provides as up-to-date a piece as he can muster with its breathy voices and synthesised momentum.

'Yum Yum' (Brock)

Brock slows proceedings to narrate the thoughts of the protagonist:

> Well, I suppose I'd better get back to my room
> And have a little lay down, I think
> And then, perhaps, something to eat

This is a playful interlude, where Brock basically repeats the children's chant of 'Yum yum yum, in my tum', over a sparse backing which simply relates to the protagonist eating the synthetic creations of the Machine rather than tasting real food. Implicit in this is the band's staunch advocacy of a vegan diet. A cry of 'All aboard!' closes proceedings, suggesting that Vashti is on her return journey.

'A Solitary Man' (Brock)

A startling and thrillingly commercial pop-rock song from Brock carries the melodic nature of the album to further heights. The only bugbear is the rather too prominent jangle of the tambourine, mollified by the all too rare appearance of Brock playing the harmonica. A single version was released and, as with most singles, it palls slightly after repetition, but it has a sturdy tune, a hummable chorus and a knack with a musical hook that is only enhanced with its added fiddle parts. Brock, however, owns the character of the protagonist a little too well as the words can clearly be read as autobiographical in their exploration of a loners' desire for solitude.

'Tube' (Brock)

Running the gamut through twinkling keyboards through to atonal crashes and clunks prepares the way for this piano-lead jaunt through rock and roll where the protagonists attempt to depart through one of the many connecting tubes that indirectly lead to the surface world. The vocals are buried in the mix, but the intent of the words is clear.

'Lost In Science' (Brock)

The Machine stops. Breaking the fourth wall slightly, Brock warns against the addictive qualities of internet culture where:

> It's sucking my soul into the virtual world
> I'm hurtling along at breakneck speed
> Buying things on e-bay that I don't really need

and then returning to the concept as the living environment breaks down and the inhabitants are forced to exit or die. In the original story, both protagonists die before they can leave the Hive, as Brock terms it, when an airship crashes into the Earth and explodes the gigantic honeycomb city. The standard Hawkwind tactic of opening on a speeding rock tune and then dissolving into an electronic haze works well here as it mirrors the disintegration of the Machine, particularly with the unrhythmic clanking at the tail end. The final waltz of the piano acts as a collapsing coda.

'Tunnels Of Darkness' (Brock/Chadwick/Hone)

Unjustly relegated to a vinyl b-side, this is a belting rock song that utterly deserves to be on the album. The trio dig in straight away, with the express rhythm, while Brock declaims the words before it morphs into singing. There is a prominent use of jazz/R&B piano which gives it a distinctive musical flavour, although there are definite musical hints of 'We Two Are One' at times. Placing a further up-tempo track on the album, especially one that provides more of the intricacies of the story, would have been a boon but here it languishes, unheard. Maybe there will be a special edition release where it is placed within the tracklisting rather than being tacked on the end as a bonus?

Conclusion

Ironically the drums on this album sound more real and live than they have in decades, just when a drum machine would have been in keeping with the synthesised, Machine-generated, story world. Maybe this is Chadwick and chums making a *Time Of The Hawklords* case for Hawkwind as musical saviours. A rapturously received tour followed and the critical and commercial fortunes of the band revived. Dead Fred dropped out after the touring had subsided, leaving an opening for a keyboard player. New band members come through in various ways: some of the road crew play in the Technicians of Spaceship Hawkwind group who have supported at various Hawkfests and HawkEaster gatherings. Mr Dibs and Haz Wheaton came through this route. Others, like Niall Hone, were recruited from the free festival and support band circuit. Magnus Martin came to the band's attention when he sold them some vegan cheese, which has to be the most unusual introduction for a band member.

Into The Woods (Cherry Red Records, May 2017)

Personnel:
Dave Brock: vocals, guitar, keyboards, synthesizer, theremin
Mr Dibs: vocals, keyboards, synthesizers
Richard Chadwick: drums, percussion, vocals
Haz Wheaton: bass, keyboards
Magnus Martin: keyboards, guitar
Big Bill Barry: guest fiddle
Produced at Earth Studios, Devon by Brockworld, 2016-2017.
Highest chart place: 34 (UK)
Running Time (approximately): 63:55

'Into The Woods' (Brock)

Partially continuing the story from the previous album, this is the start of a different journey. The hero has died but others, the Homeless, have already broken free of the restrictions of their underground life and are settling on the Earth under a real sky, feeling like pioneers. Musically quoting a piano passage from 'Hall of the Mountain Grill' and then charging into a savage metal riff gets the album off to a flying start. Taking the form of a caution to anyone who dares enter, the lyrics make it plain:

> Into the woods we run and hide
> There's no escape, you can't survive
> We'll tear your flesh
> And eat your bones

The warning appears to be about vicious woodland sprites, especially given the vocal treatment, that lie in wait for the unwary.

'Cottage In The Woods' (Brock)

A gentler counterbalance to the opening song, this measured trudge finds our narrator hiding in his cottage, lonely and scared of the denizens of the forest. Hardly a rural idyll, this has become a solitary fortress against the dark.

'The Woodpecker' (Brock/Chadwick)
A ridiculous piece that, well, imitates the sound of a woodpecker…

'Have You Seen Them?' (Brock/Chadwick/Darbyshire/Haz Wheaton)
A blazingly catchy descending guitar riff immediately wipes the last track away with a commercially potent musical hook allied to a decent chorus. Chadwick's vocals are ragged but tuneful, and they suit the organic nature of the album theme. The printed lyrics miss out two verses and the song is definitely overstretched by several minutes in its jagged chord propulsion middle eight but that superb riff conquers everything, even Wheaton's solo section and the bloated end piece. A cut down single mix would be amazing.

'Ascent' (Brock)
Originally a *Brockworld* solo song, this has been slowed down and folked up for this largely acoustic musing on the failings of the human race to protect the seas and the Earth. It seems to have been rearranged purely to fit into the increasingly dapper acoustic sets that the band are performing and it improves upon the earlier recording, while still packing a lyrical chorus:

> In this world of avarice, greed and hate
> We must turn the tide and educate

'Space Ship Blues' (Brock/Chadwick/Wheaton)
Someone, somewhere, is going to have a fit at this *radical* reworking of 'Nuclear Drive' from the always weirdly popular *Church of Hawkwind*. Pausing only to wind up the audio generator, the band throw themselves into a blast of Cajun madness that reveals the inevitable banjo and fiddle accompaniment but also finds room for some mad country and western harmonies, a theremin and the jaw harp that Calvert used so long ago. If a bizarre space hoedown appeals to you, here it is!

'The Wind' (Brock/Chadwick/Wheaton)
A piece of audio verite that includes the woodpecker effects, actual bird noises and woodland ambience married to a spoken word piece which eventually blunders into something rhythmic, even if it isn't musical.

'Vegan Lunch' (Brock)
A jerky rhythm and a buried vocal don't exactly help the message of this pro-vegan trifle. It occupies a little too much time for its half-formed musical idea and the lyrics, while worthy, are neither anthemic nor memorable. Here ends the sagging middle portion of the album.

'Magic Scenes' (Brock/Chadwick/Wheaton)
Twirling synthesizers and a throbbing bass are the hooks for this breathless return to form, with Brock singing with gusto and providing a lively guitar break to elevate the mood, even if it slightly stretches beyond its natural life.

'Darkland' (Darbyshire)
Dibs goes for the melancholy acoustic guitar and fiddle option here, with a two minute instrumental that carries the sorrowful mood of the album onward.

'Wood Nymph' (Brock/Chadwick/Wheaton)
Another nod at folk-rock music, in that inimitable Hawkwind way, which recounts the nostalgic story of a chance meeting with this forest spirit and draws an unexpectedly emotive vocal from Brock. The fiddle again makes its mark here, but there is no hint of American country in this Albion-to-the-core tale.

> My breath is leaving, I'm old and grey
> I have my dreams of that eventful day

Listeners could be forgiven for thinking this is autobiographical.

'Deep Cavern' (Darbyshire)
Riding roughshod over the printed lyrics, this slow thud seems submerged in ancient folk stories and mulling on the concept of time, all while magpies cackle and Dibs talks of them knowing 'your name'. There seems to be a *Mythago Wood* (Robert Holdstock's fictional examination of fairy tales) concept peeping out from behind the cover of the album, but it never gets going.

'Magic Mushrooms' (Brock/Chadwick/Wheaton)
Crashing straight into the last track, literally, this thundering semi-jam sounds almost live, and definitely harks back to the very old days with its punishing rhythm, repeated riff and heads down attack. There is a brief breather before the band charge on again, boisterously echoing the chunky guitars and bare-knuckle improvisation that started the band in the first place. What on earth it has to do with magic mushrooms, however, is unclear.

More Line-Up Changes

The unexpected loss of Haz Wheaton and Mr Dibs after the *Road To Utopia* acoustic re-arrangements album meant that Brock needed a fast replacement who knew the songs well. Niall Hone was therefore recalled to the line-up to play the excellent orchestral dates that had been set up to promote the album, and the newly reconstituted band found themselves inspired to start more recording almost straight away. Initially conceptual (about the annihilation of the human race and aliens travelling across the cosmos feasting off all other life forms) the band opted to complete the album rather than get bogged down in the intricacies of a storyline.

All Aboard The Skylark (Cherry Red Records, October 2019)

Personnel:
Dave Brock: vocals, guitar, keyboards, synthesizer, bass
Richard Chadwick: drums, percussion, vocals
Niall Hone: guitar, keyboards, synthesizer, bass, vocals
Magnus Martin: guitar, keyboards, vocals
Produced at Earth Studios, Devon by Hawkwind, 2018-2019.
Highest chart place: 34 (UK)
Running Time (approximately): 42:24

'Flesh Fondue' (Brock)

A radical remake of 1981's 'Star Cannibal', this surges into life with a spectacular riff, a swerving rhythm and a thick, syrupy sound that echoes Hawkwind's earliest years. Briefly bringing to mind 'Uncle Sam's On Mars', this triumphantly reintroduces Hone and his remarkably solid bass playing. The weighty undertow to this song is heartening although it contrasts awkwardly with the space jazz coda.

Brock provides bravura vocals to this gleeful ode to aliens who eat their conquered prey and it startlingly updates a previously limp tune, beginning the album in fine style. Vegan he may be, but Brock chews the lyrics like the extra-terrestrials munch down on their foes, and he relishes every nibbled nuance.

'Nets Of Space' (Brock)

A sterling space rock instrumental that belies its single author, this sweeps along with great aplomb based on a mid-paced drum pattern and threatens to explode into life but never quite achieves its potential. The heavily treated and distorted speech popping up partway through is unintelligible, but suggests that the aliens are talking with their mouths full.

'Last Man On Earth' (Magnus Martin)

Martin throws in a largely acoustic song for his first full writing appearance, and it rather reveals the lack of character in his voice as it strains to keep up with the demands of the tune. The marvellous coda of harmony voices and the instrumental aftermath make up for a lot of the flatness of the earlier verses and choruses. That ending has 'singalong' written all over it and it seems to have been expressly written for the acoustic sets that pepper the bands current live outings. Audible through the folk haze, is the first appearance of Michal Sosna's lilting saxophone, implying, once and for all, that any reconciliation with Nik Turner is long past.

Lyrically this is about the last man returning to Earth and finding it bountiful, after the depredations of the alien flesh-eaters, rather than devastated. Martin appears to have been heavily inspired by Richard Matheson's masterful novel *I Am Legend* with its depiction of the last living man on Earth being surrounded by, in that case, 'vampires'. The parallels are plain and show Martin's great taste in literature.

'We Are Not Dead... Only Sleeping' (Brock)
Rolling effortlessly into life this is a melodic tale of the revivification of the Skylark's crew, who are coming out of suspended animation. Breathily echoing their slow rise to consciousness, the chorale voices and loping beat are only interrupted by a jazz piano trifle that merely adds to the mood. Unlike previous albums, this is another song that doesn't outstay its welcome and is all the more memorable for that.

'All Aboard The Skylark' (Brock/Chadwick/Hone/Martin)
An instrumental title track that suggests the band were gelling in the studio and jammed this tune before smartening it up with overdubs and production curls. Michal Sosna reappears in full-on Turner squealing mode, although it all fades out rather than opens up, which is a shame.

Is Polish Michal Sosna any relation to saxophonist Rudolf Sosna of German krautrock anarchists Faust? I would like to think so.

'65 Million Years Ago' (Brock)
Brock plunders his revitalised store of melodic mid-tempo rock songs with this eruption of tectonic proportions detailing the cataclysmic death of the dinosaurs and the cycle that lead to the creation of mammalian life. Brock renders a committed vocal and returns to the delightful harmony singing that seems to characterise this album.

'In The Beginning' (Brock)
This is an almost hummable ambient space rock instrumental that sounds like Brock's solo work but fits in with the music surrounding it.

'The Road To...' (Brock)
A full band instrumental, which flows nicely (although the fake finger-clicking could have been excised) and features some nice guitar soloing along with a further appearance of the jazz piano styling's that haunt the album. Again, utilising Brock's hitherto buried sense of melody, this slows the album down in time for the somewhat epic ending.

'The Fantasy Of Faldum' (Martin)
This sprawling, acoustic rock-based finale was inspired by the 1916 Hermann

Hesse fairy tale *Faldum,* which ends with an aged and philosophical living mountain observing the collapse of the land upon which Faldum once stood, and its own disintegration, and accepting the eventual encroachment of the sea and the ultimate indifference of nature. Lyrically, it provides a fitting end to an album concerned with the cyclical cataclysms that befall every planet, including the Earth. This is a lot to pack into one song, even one with a nine-minute running time.

Martin pitches the vocal melody at a more comfortable level for his voice and proves a capable interpreter of his own song. All the players get to shine, but the song cannot really support its length, even with the changes of momentum involved. The giveaway to the somewhat bloated running time is that the verses are all repeated several times. The track is a partial failure, but Martin is only beginning his songwriting career and there is plenty of time for him to create wondrous material.

And Finally ...

The current ship shows absolutely no sign of slowing down, with a triumphant 50th Anniversary tour, featuring the energetic return of the always entertaining Tim Blake, and a surprisingly sprightly and consistent album. Dave Brock is now 78, at the time of writing, and thankfully shows every sign of captaining the ship for years to come. Surely he must be the oldest working rock star not just touring a nostalgia show but continuing to innovate and record new and incisive material.

Bibliography

Abrahams, Ian. *Hawkwind: Sonic Assassins* SAF Publishing (UK), 2004.
Buckley, Peter, ed. *The Rough Guide To Rock: 3rd edition* Rough Guides (UK), 2003.
Butterworth, Michael. *Time Of The Hawklords* Star Books (UK), 1976.
Butterworth, Michael. *Queens Of Deliria* Star Books (UK), 1977.
Butterworth, Michael and Walker, Bob. *Ledge Of Darkness* Collector's Guide Publishing (Ontario), 1994.
Christopulos, Jim and Smart, Phil. *Van Der Graaf Generator - The Book: a history of the band Van Der Graaf Generator 1967 to 1978* 'Phil and Jim' (UK), 2005.
Clerk, Carol. *The Saga Of Hawkwind: updated edition* Omnibus Press (UK), 2006.
Collins, Jeff. *Rock Legends at Rockfield* University of Wales Press (UK), 2007.
Cope, Julian. *Krautrocksampler: One Head's Guide to the Great Kosmiche Musik - 1968 Onwards: 3rd edition* Head Heritage (UK), 1996.
Fane-Saunders, Kilmeny, ed. *Radio Times Guide To Science Fiction* BBC Worldwide Limited (UK), 2001
Fitch, Vernon. *The Pink Floyd Encyclopedia: 3rd edition* Collector's Guide Publishing (Ontario), 2005.
Godwin, Robert. *The Illustrated Collector's Guide To Hawkwind* Collector's Guide Publishing (Ontario), 1993.
Kilmister, Ian and Garza, Janiss. *Lemmy: White Line Fever* Simon & Schuster (UK), 2002.
Manning, Toby. *The Rough Guide To Pink Floyd* Rough Guides (London), 2006.
Moorcock, Michael and Greenland, Colin. *Michael Moorcock: Death Is No Obstacle* Savoy Books (Manchester), 1992.
Moore, Alan. *Wind Power* (Hawkwind interview) Sounds newspaper (London), November 11 1982.
Strong, Martin C. *The Essential Rock Discography* Canongate Books (Edinburgh), 2006.
Tait, Kris. *This Is Hawkwind, Do Not Panic* Hawkwind (UK), 1988 edition.
Turner, Nik and Thompson, Dave. *The Spirit of Hawkwind 1969-1976* Cleopatra Press (Los Angeles), 2015.
Wade, Chris with Garbutt, Paul. *The Music of Hawkwind* Wisdom Twins Books (UK), 2016.

Hawkwind Contacts, Internet Sites

Hawkfan
www.hawkwind.com
www.starfarer.net was a fan repository of considerable size and depth that is now, sadly, defunct.

On Track series

Queen – Andrew Wild 978-1-78952-003-3
Emerson Lake and Palmer – Mike Goode 978-1-78952-000-2
Deep Purple and Rainbow 1968-79 – Steve Pilkington 978-1-78952-002-6
Yes – Stephen Lambe 978-1-78952-001-9
Blue Oyster Cult – Jacob Holm-Lupo 978-1-78952-007-1
The Beatles – Andrew Wild 978-1-78952-009-5
Roy Wood and the Move – James R Turner 978-1-78952-008-8
Genesis – Stuart MacFarlane 978-1-78952-005-7
JethroTull – Jordan Blum 978-1-78952-016-3
The Rolling Stones 1963-80 – Steve Pilkington 978-1-78952-017-0
Judas Priest – John Tucker 978-1-78952-018-7
Toto – Jacob Holm-Lupo 978-1-78952-019-4
Van Der Graaf Generator – Dan Coffey 978-1-78952-031-6
Frank Zappa 1966 to 1979 – Eric Benac 978-1-78952-033-0
Elton John in the 1970s – Peter Kearns 978-1-78952-034-7
The Moody Blues – Geoffrey Feakes 978-1-78952-042-2
The Beatles Solo 1969-1980 – Andrew Wild 978-1-78952-030-9
Steely Dan – Jez Rowden 978-1-78952-043-9
Hawkwind – Duncan Harris 978-1-78952-052-1
Fairport Convention – Kevan Furbank 978-1-78952-051-4
Iron Maiden – Steve Pilkington 978-1-78952-061-3
Dream Theater – Jordan Blum 978-1-78952-050-7
10CC – Peter Kearns 978-1-78952-054-5
Gentle Giant – Gary Steel 978-1-78952-058-3
Kansas – Kevin Cummings 978-1-78952-057-6
Mike Oldfield – Ryan Yard 978-1-78952-060-6
The Who – Geoffrey Feakes 978-1-78952-076-7

On Screen series

Carry On... – Stephen Lambe 978-1-78952-004-0
Powell and Pressburger – Sam Proctor 978-1-78952-013-2
Seinfeld Seasons 1 to 5 – Stephen Lambe 978-1-78952-012-5
Francis Ford Coppola – Cam Cobb and Stephen Lambe 978-1-78952-022-4
Monty Python – Steve Pilkington 978-1-78952-047-7
Doctor Who: The David Tennant Years – Jamie Hailstone 978-1-78952-066-8
James Bond – Andrew Wild 978-1-78952-010-1

Other Books

Not As Good As The Book – Andy Tillison 978-1-78952-021-7
The Voice. Frank Sinatra in the 1940s – Stephen Lambe 978-1-78952-032-3
Maximum Darkness – Deke Leonard 978-1-78952-048-4
The Twang Dynasty – Deke Leonard 978-1-78952-049-1
Maybe I Should've Stayed In Bed – Deke Leonard 978-1-78952-053-8
Tommy Bolin: In and Out of Deep Purple – Laura Shenton 978-1-78952-070-5
Jon Anderson and the Warriors - the road to Yes – David Watkinson 978-1-78952-059-0

and many more to come!

Would you like to write for Sonicbond Publishing?

At Sonicbond Publishing we are always on the look-out for authors, particularly for our two main series:

On Track. Mixing fact with in depth analysis, the On Track series examines the work of a particular musical artist or group. All genres are considered from easy listening and jazz to 60s soul to 90s pop, via rock and metal.

On Screen. This series looks at the world of film and television. Subjects considered include directors, actors and writers, as well as entire television and film series. As with the On Track series, we balance fact with analysis.

While professional writing experience would, of course, be an advantage the most important qualification is to have real enthusiasm and knowledge of your subject. First-time authors are welcomed, but the ability to write well in English is essential.

Sonicbond Publishing has distribution throughout Europe and North America, and all books are also published in E-book form. Authors will be paid a royalty based on sales of their book.

Further details are available from www.sonicbondpublishing.co.uk. To contact us, complete the contact form there or email info@sonicbondpublishing.co.uk